ISLAND HOME

TIM WINTON

ISLAND HOME

a landscape memoir

MILKWEED EDITIONS

Published 2017 by Milkweed Editions
Printed in the United States of America
Cover design by John Canty © Penguin Australia Pty Ltd
Cover photograph by Photogerson
Author photo by Hank Kordas
Interior design by Samantha Jayaweera, Penguin Australia Pty Ltd
Interior illustrations by Mali Moir
The text of this book is set in Adobe Garamond Pro.
17 18 19 20 21   5 4 3 2 1
First US Edition

Milkweed Editions, an independent nonprofit publisher, gratefully acknowledges sustaining
support from the Jerome Foundation; the Lindquist & Vennum Foundation; the McKnight
Foundation; the National Endowment for the Arts; the Target Foundation; and other generous
contributions from foundations, corporations, and individuals. Also, this activity is made
possible by the voters of Minnesota through a Minnesota State Arts Board Operating Support
grant, thanks to a legislative appropriation from the arts and cultural heritage fund, and a grant
from the Wells Fargo Foundation. For a full listing of Milkweed Editions supporters, please
visit milkweed.org.

Library of Congress Cataloging-in-Publication Data
Names: Winton, Tim, author.
Title: Island home : a landscape memoir / Tim Winton.
Description: Minneapolis, Minnesota : Milkweed Editions, 2017. | A reissue of the edition published in
Melbourne, Vic. (Hamish Hamilton, an imprint of Penguin Books, 2015). Identifiers: LCCN 2017002185
(print) | LCCN 2017006385 (ebook) | ISBN 9781571311245 (paperback) | ISBN 9781571319586 (ebook)
Subjects: LCSH: Winton, Tim. | Authors, Australian--20th century--Biography. | Landscapes--
Australia. | Landscapes in literature. | Australia--Description and travel. | BISAC: BIOGRAPHY
& AUTOBIOGRAPHY / Personal Memoirs. | TRAVEL / Australia & Oceania. | NATURE /
Environmental Conservation & Protection. Classification: LCC PR9619.3.W585 Z95 2017 (print) |
LCC PR9619.3.W585 (ebook) | DDC 828/.91403 [B] --dc23
LC record available at https://lccn.loc.gov/2017002185

Milkweed Editions is committed to ecological stewardship. We strive to align our book
production practices with this principle, and to reduce the impact of our operations in
the environment. We are a member of the Green Press Initiative, a nonprofit coalition of
publishers, manufacturers, and authors working to protect the world's endangered forests and
conserve natural resources. *Island Home* was printed on acid-free 100% postconsumer-waste
paper by Edwards Brothers Malloy.

for Hannah Rachel Bell

Turn home, the sun goes down; swimmer, turn home.

JUDITH WRIGHT,
'The Surfer'

My island home is waiting for me.

NEIL MURRAY,
'My Island Home'

I

County Offaly, 1988

Black sky down around our ears, my son and I climb the stile in the frigid, buffeting wind. Hail slants in, pinging and peppering us. Neither the hedge nor the adjoining drystone wall offers much protection so we press on up the long, lumpy field toward the cottage and the waiting fire.

Only moments ago the black slates and white chimney were plain against the crest of the hill; now everything but the tussocks at our feet is obscured by the squall belting down the valley. I expect my boy to be cowed by the stinging ice and the suddenly savage afternoon but he seems enchanted. He's nearly four years old. The short, dull day has finally delivered some excitement. Waving his knobby stick like a marauding buccaneer, he swashbuckles uphill in his little orange wellies, and together we inadvertently ambush a large hare. The creature has been hunched in the hail-harried grass and for several moments it can only gaze up at us in terror. Finally it bolts. It zigzags up the incline from one tuft to the next. We look at each other a moment, the boy and I, and then with piratical hoots we give chase.

Later by the fire he sets aside his hot chocolate to stare at the snapshots of home pinned to the wall. All the sun-creased faces of friends and family. Daggy hats and bare chests. Dogs in utes. The endless clear space behind people, the towering skies and open horizons. He lingers over the dreamy white beaches and mottled limestone reefs at low tide, sculpted dunes at sunset.

'Is it real?' he asks, cheeks rosy, hair in cockscombs from the towel.

'Of course,' I tell him, startled. 'Don't you remember? Look. That's Granma. There's Shaz.'

But he fingers the sky and sea behind our loved ones as if the reality he once knew is now so distant, so unlike where we are, as to seem untrustworthy.

'It's home,' I say. 'Remember? That's Australia.'

It's only been a year but that's a big chunk of the kid's short life and already home has begun to seem fantastic. Before this we were in Paris, which was lovely, though it was all hard surfaces and primly divided space. There were wondrous tunnels, cobbles and curvy walls, tiny cars and hurtling underground trains, but so many open expanses were barred and fenced off and it was hard for him to meet other children. The bourgeois kids in the neighbourhood were either strapped in and pushed along by au pairs or driven afoot in herds by barking teachers. At the weekends infants were paraded and brandished in cafés like fashion accessories, testimony to the good taste and excellent Gallic genes of their parents. Indoors these kids may have been urban gentry, but outside they looked like vassals. In Paris, playing on the grass was illegal. The only unscheduled social encounters took place in the queue for the carousel in the local square, or within the confines of a white-gravelled playground that was corralled like a saleyard. Kids who were unacquainted eyed each other off at a distance.

In many ways Paris was an easy city to be in. There was beauty everywhere you looked. We'd never lived in an apartment before, and having to contend with the sounds and smells of others so close above and beside us was strange and exciting. But as winter set in and the fountains froze in candied cascades and we were forced to retreat indoors, there was something pent up in our little boy that couldn't be ignored. I felt it in myself, this churning agitation, and didn't understand it until months later, running madly uphill in an Irish hailstorm. For while I'd assumed our mounting mutual fractiousness was the result of cultural fatigue – the perpetual bafflement at local customs and manners – the real source was physical confinement and an absence of wildness.

As the big storm ripped overhead my wife came in and sat by the fire. She ruffled our son's hair and gave me a quizzical look. It was as if she'd instantly registered the change of mood.

'When we get home,' the boy declared, 'we're getting a dog. In a ute.'

Later that night, as he slept in his loft, we spoke at length about his little declaration. We knew what he hankered for wasn't really a pet, or the car it came in, but what they stood for – his Australian life. And the wild spaces that made it possible.

The island seen and felt

I grew up on the world's largest island. The bald fact slips from consciousness so easily I'm obliged to remind myself now and again. But in an age when a culture examines itself primarily through politics and ideology, perhaps my forgetting something so basic should come as no surprise. Our minds are often elsewhere. The material facts of life, the organic and concrete forces that fashion us, are overlooked as if they're irrelevant or even mildly embarrassing. Our creaturely existence is registered, measured, discussed and represented in increasingly abstract terms. Maybe this helps explain how someone like me, who should know better, can forget he's an islander. Australia the place is constantly overshadowed by Australia the national idea, Australia the economic enterprise. There's no denying the power of these conceits. I've been shaped by them. But they are hardly the only forces at work. I'm increasingly mindful of the degree to which geography, distance and weather have moulded my sensory palate, my imagination and expectations. The island continent has not been mere background. Landscape has exerted a kind of force upon me that is every bit as geological as family. Like many Australians, I feel this tectonic grind – call it a familial ache – most keenly when abroad.

Living in Europe in the 1980s I made the mistake of assuming that what separated me from citizens of the Old World was only language and history, as if I really was the mongrel European transplant of my formal education. But I hadn't given my own geography sufficient credit. Neither, of course, had those who taught me. It wasn't simply about what I'd read or not read – my physical response to new places unsettled me. It was as if my body were in rebellion. Outside the great cities and the charming villages of the Old World, I felt that all my wiring was scrambled. Where I had expected to appreciate the monuments and love the natural environment, the reality was entirely the reverse. The immense beauty of many buildings and streetscapes had an immediate and visceral impact, and yet in the natural world, where I am generally most comfortable, I was hesitant. While I was duly impressed by what I saw, I could never connect bodily and emotionally. Being from a flat, dry continent I looked forward to the prospect of soaring alps and thundering rivers, lush valleys and fertile plains, and yet when I actually beheld them I was puzzled by how muted my responses were. My largely Eurocentric education had prepared me for a sense of recognition I did not feel, and this was confounding. The paintings and poems about all these places still moved me, so I couldn't understand the queer impatience that crept up when I saw them in real time and space. Weren't these landforms and panoramas beautiful? Well, yes, of course they were, although a little bit of them seemed to go a long way. To someone from an austere landscape they often looked too cute; they were pretty, even saccharine. I had a nagging sensation that I wasn't 'getting it'.

In the first instance I struggled with scale. In Europe the dimensions of physical space seemed compressed. The looming vertical presence of mountains cut me off from the horizon. I'd not lived with that kind of spatial curtailment before. Even a city of skyscrapers is more porous than a snowcapped range. Alps form a solid barrier, an obstacle every bit as conceptual as visual and physical. Alpine bluffs and crags don't just rear up, they lean outward, projecting their mass, and their solidity does not relent. For a West Australian like me, whose default setting is in diametric opposition, and for whom space is the impinging force, the effect is claustrophobic. I think I was constantly and instinctively searching for distances that were unavailable, measuring space and coming up short.

The second and more significant thing to unsettle me was that every landform bore the inescapable mark of culture and technology. Of course even remotest Australia shows the signature of human activity – ancient fire regimes have shaped habitats and there are paintings and petroglyphs in places that seem at a glance to have been forever unpeopled – but many Aboriginal adjustments, amendments and embellishments are so discreet they hardly register as impositions; in fact to the unschooled eye they are invisible. In Europe, however, the most dramatic and apparently solitary landscapes are unmistakably modified. Around every mountain pass and bend it seems there is another tunnel, a funicular, a fashionable resort or a rash of reflective signage.

It took a while to understand that the source of my mounting dismay was a simple lack of relief from my own kind. I had never encountered places so relentlessly denatured. Above the snowline there was always a circling helicopter, and beyond that a tracery of jet contrails attesting to the thousands travelling the skies at every moment of the day and night. Down in the valleys and along the impossibly fertile plains, nature was only visible through the overlaid embroidery of the people who'd brought it to heel. Whether I was in France, Ireland, Holland or the more rugged Greece, it seemed that every field, hedge and well was named, apportioned and accounted for. It was a vista of almost unrelieved enclosure and domestication. Those rare spaces not fully inhabited or exploited were unambiguously altered. Where once there'd been forests there were now only woods. Conservation reserves were more like sculpted parks than remnant, self-generated ecosystems. Even the northern sky looked colonized, its curdled atmosphere a constant and depressing reminder of human dominion. As a boy I'd viewed the sky as a clear and overwatching lens, but at my lowest homesick moments in Europe that same eye looked sick and occluded.

On bright days the light was slate-blue, pretty in a painterly sort of way, and heartening after such long periods of gloom, but it lacked the white-hot charge my body and spirit yearned for. I was calibrated differently to a European.

In a seedy cinema on the rue du Temple, watching Disney's *Peter Pan* with my son, I found that although we were all gazing at the same screen in the flickering dark, I was seeing a different film to the rest of the audience. What seemed fantastical and exotic to the Parisian kids looked like home to me. I knew secret coves and hidey-holes like those of the Lost Boys. I'd grown up in a world of rocky islands, boats and obscuring bush. To my mind the only setting that was alien – even whimsical – was the cold, lonely nursery in the Darling family attic. The wild opportunity of Neverland with its freedom from adult surveillance was deeply, warmly familiar. Watching the movie for the umpteenth time and seeing it anew, forsaking story and focusing greedily on the backdrop, I understood what a complete stranger I was in that hemisphere. But acknowledging my strangeness made those years abroad easier to digest and enjoy.

When I was born in 1960 there was about a square

kilometre for every person on the island continent. Fifty-five years later the population has doubled, but density is still exceptionally low. Despite a peopled history of sixty thousand years, Australia remains a place with more land than people, more geography than architecture. But it is not and never has been empty. Since people first walked out of Africa and made their way down to this old chunk of Gondwana when it was not yet so distant from Asia and the rest of the world, it has been explored and inhabited, modified and mythologized, walked and sung. People were chanting and dancing and painting here tens and tens of thousand of years before the advent of the toga and the sandal. This is true antiquity. Few landscapes have been so deeply known. And fewer still have been so lightly inhabited.

People learnt to live differently here because circumstances were unique. Instead of four seasons there were five, sometimes six. Water was scarce. The soils were thin and infertile and the plants and animals were like nothing else on earth. Living here was a specialized affair. Australia is hatched and laced with ancient story and human experience, and yet there has always been a lot of space between these gossamer threads of culture. They are strong but so unifyingly taut as to be hard to distinguish, especially by those who go looking for signs of building or evidence of perennial habitation.

Those who became the Aboriginal peoples of this continent were almost always required to live nomadically. Their occupation of many regions was seasonal, even notional. Distant but precious country was held by skeins of song and webs of ritual, so even country that was not physically occupied was never empty. Places were intimately known and culturally vital but culture rarely imposed itself in concrete terms. Artifacts and constructions were largely ephemeral and icons required seasonal refreshment. Just as a child was 'conceived' by appearing as an image in a waterhole before a woman became pregnant, culture originated in and deferred to country.

Two centuries after this way of living was disrupted forever, Australia is still a place where there is more landscape than culture. Our island resists the levels of containment and permanent physical presence that prevail on most other continents. It probably always will.

I'm not saying Australia has no culture or that its cultural life is inconsiderable. But most Asian and European countries can be defined in human terms. Mention of India, China, Italy, France or Germany will quickly bring to mind human actions and artifacts, but at first blush

Australia connotes something non-human. Of course the genius of indigenous culture is unquestionable, but even this is overshadowed by the scale and insistence of the land that inspired it. Geography trumps all. Its logic underpins everything. And after centuries of European settlement it persists, for no post-invasion achievement, no city nor soaring monument can compete with the grandeur of the land. Don't think this is a romantic notion. Everything we do in this country is still overborne and underwritten by the seething tumult of nature. An opera house, an iron bridge, a tinsel-topped tower – these are creative marvels, but as structures they look pretty feeble against the landscape in which they stand. Think of the brooding mass and ever-changing face of Uluru. Will architects ever make stone live like this? Consider the bewildering scale and complexity of Purnululu, otherwise known as the Bungle Bungles. It's like a cryptic megacity wrought by engineers on peyote. Humans are unlikely to ever manufacture anything as beautiful and intricate.

Few visitors to these shores arrive seeking the built glories of our culture. Generally they're here for wildness, to experience space in a way that's unavailable, and sometimes unimaginable, in countries where there is more culture than landscape. I'm no self-hating utopian. And giving the natural world its due does not make you a misanthrope. I've spent my life in the pursuit and maintenance of culture. I'm in awe of the uncanny brilliance of humans. I love being in the great cities of the world. And it's true – some buildings are gifts rather than impositions. But I am antipodean enough, and perhaps of sufficient age, to wonder now and then whether architecture is, in the end, what you console yourself with once wild landscape has been subsumed.

Space was my primary inheritance. I was formed by gaps, nurtured in the long pauses between people. I'm part of a thin and porous human culture through which the land slants in, seen or felt, at every angle: for each mechanical noise, five natural sounds; for every built structure a landform twice as large and twenty times as complex. And over it all, an impossibly open sky, dwarfing everything.

In the semi-arid range country where I live these days the heavens draw you out, like a multidimensional horizon. For most of the year the arrival of a cloud is something of an event. Along the south coast where I spent my adolescence, the air boils with gothic clouds. There the sky's commotion renders you so feverish your thoughts are closer to music than language. In the desert the night sky sucks at you, star by star, galaxy by galaxy, until you begin to feel you could fall out into it at any moment. In Australia the sky is not the safe enclosing canopy it appears to be elsewhere. It's the scantiest membrane imaginable, barely sufficient as a barrier between earthbound creatures and eternity. Standing alone at dawn on the Nullarbor, or out on a saltpan the size of a small country, you feel a twinge of terror because the sky seems to go on forever. It has perilous depths and oceanic movements. In our hemisphere the sky stops you in your tracks, derails your thoughts, unmoors you from what you were doing before it got you by the collar. No wonder Australian painters, from the Kimberley's Jarinyanu David Downs to Tasmania's Philip Wolfhagen, continue to treat it as a worthy subject, despite the frustrations of some critics who expect them to move on to something a little more 'sophisticated', by which they mean untainted by the specifics of place. For some islanders the weight of particularity is too great to bear. They spurn the bounded isolation of Tasmania, Lord Howe, the Torres Strait or the so-called mainland and seek refuge in cosmopolitanism, and who could blame them? Australians have long felt this push and pull. Moated in by oceans, sharing no borders, they become curious, restless, oppressed by the relentless familiarity of their surroundings. When you're on an island the grass will always be greener elsewhere because it can't be glimpsed across the frontier. You're mentally greening

places that are oceans away. Islanders can't help but conjure distant paradises for themselves. Australians are great
travellers. You meet them as expatriates all over the world.
Now and then you still encounter those of the old school
who are touchy about self-exile, as if their countrymen
disapprove of them the way they might have in the 1950s.
The most defensive among them despise those who stayed
home, and it's instructive and quite moving to watch some
return in late life to mend bridges, uncertain if it's home
that's become more congenial or something in themselves
that's deepened with time.

There is no denying the fact that there's something physically relentless about Australia, but there's also something
hauntingly paradoxical, for to even the most reverent
observer it sometimes feels as if this continent is more
air than matter, more pause than movement, more space
than time. The place is still itself. It continues to impose. It
imprints itself upon the body, and in order to make sense of
it the mind is constantly struggling to catch up. This is why,
despite the postmodern and nearly post-physical age we live
and work in, Australian writers and painters continue to
obsess about landscape. It's not that we are laggards. We are
in a place where the material facts of life must still be con-
tended with. There is so much more of it than us. We are

forever battling to come to terms. The encounter between ourselves and the land is a live concern. Elsewhere this story is largely done and dusted, with nature in stumbling retreat, but here our life in nature remains an open question and how we answer it will define not just our culture and politics but our very survival.

To be a writer preoccupied with landscape is to accept a weird and constant tension between the indoors and the outdoors. I am so thin-skinned about weather and so eager for physical sensation I seem to spend a shameful amount of energy fretting and plotting escape, like a schoolboy. Sat near a window as a pupil, I was a dead loss. And I'm not much different now. I can't even hang a painting in my workroom, for what else is a painting but a window? My thoughts are drawn outward; I'm entranced. Which is a romantic way of saying I'm mentally bogged to the boards. So a lot of the time I write in a blank cubicle, my back to the view. Which means I spend quite a bit of the day getting up to leave the room, to stand outside in the sunlight for a minute, sniffing the wind, looking at the sky. It's like the compulsive adjusting of a valve. On occasion I feel better for having done so. The rest of the time I regret it. The grown-up in me concedes that at least I've had a taste of the day. But the kid within can only feel more keenly what he's missed.

Now and then, of course, I just bolt. I pile a few chattels into the Land Cruiser and hit the road. I drive until sunset and then pull over in a different state of mind, or even another state of the Federation altogether. There's often no purpose to these trips beyond the joy of being in the open, unrolling a swag in a creekbed or in a hollow between dunes, sitting by a fire and watching the stars come out like gooseflesh in the heavens. These headlong excursions begin as flights from enclosure and I know they sound like escapes, but to me they're more like calls answered. Within moments of leaving, once I've achieved some momentum, it's as if I'm subject to a homing impulse I barely understand. Lying under the night sky I feel a curious sense of return and restoration, not unlike the way I felt as a kid coming in the back door to the sudsy smell of the laundry and the parental mutter of the tub filling down the hall.

Still, going home is not always a cosy business. It can be harsh and bewildering. The places dearest to me can be really hard to reach. They're austere, savage, unpredictable. And like taciturn cousins and leery in-laws they don't always come out and say what they mean. They give you the stink-eye at breakfast and do what they can to make your stay uncomfortable. You arrive moody and distracted, unprepared for the complexity of the family dynamics, wrongfooted from the get-go. Not much of our country is lush or instantly congenial. The regions I know best are particularly challenging and my home range in the west can be hard work – it's spiky, dry, irritating, even humiliating, and after some visits I often feel as spent and dismayed as any guest at a Christmas lunch, wondering why the hell I bothered. But homecomings are partly about submitting to the uncomfortably familiar, aren't they? Like a hapless adult child, you go back for more, despite yourself, eternally trying to figure out the family puzzle. Even so you get sustenance, just from trying, by remaining open to the mystery, suspecting that if you give up on it you'll be left with nothing.

This country leans in on you. It weighs down hard. Like family. To my way of thinking, it *is* family.

I have spent a lot of time watching Australians do this filial dance with landscape. Urban and prosperous as they are, living beyond the constraints of weather and nature in a way their forebears could never have imagined, many seek to engage in an almost ritual, if contradictory, pre-occupation with the outdoors, spending a fortune each year on off-road vehicles, caravans, campers and adventure equipment. Some of this is mere fetish, some is purely aspirational, but millions of people are still eager to be out hiking, climbing, camping, kayaking, fishing, surfing, sailing or exploring the first chance they get. It's not simply a matter of escaping the indoor servitude of working life. There is a palpable outward urge, a searching impulse, something embedded in our physical culture, our sensory make-up. It speaks of an implicit collective understanding that the land is still present at the corner of our eye, still *out there*, but also carried within, as a genetic connection. You don't need to lurk in a camping store to pick up on this vernacular assumption. Half an hour at a suburban barbecue will suffice. You see it in people's behaviour as much as in what they utter. It's down hard and deep like the taproot of a half-forgotten tree, and it shows no sign of withering away. For despite how cossetted and manicured and airconditioned contemporary life has become, the land remains a tantalizing and watchful presence over our shoulder. We've imbibed it unwittingly; it's in our bones like a sacramental ache. Waiting for us. Even if only as an impending absence. If such a yearning wasn't real advertisers wouldn't spend billions of dollars taunting us with it. Behold the glory of Kakadu, they tell us, the endless beaches of Fraser Island, the blood-red breakaways of Karijini, the darkling mysteries of the Tarkine, the miracle of Lake Eyre in flood. And here, of course, is the vehicle to get you there, the shoes to wear when you arrive, the drink you need to celebrate having made the effort. To sell something disposable they need to set it against something truly substantial and enduring. And in Australia what is more impressive than the land? Culturally, psychologically, it's still the gold standard.

No matter how we live, and what we think of ourselves, the sublimated facts of our physical situation are ever-present, and as moving water grinds stones into fresh and often unlikely shapes, the land presses in, forever wearing, pushing, honing. Most of the time we barely register the attrition. In a disembodied era of digital technology and franchise culture there are periods when even an Australian at home can feel he or she might be anyplace, or perhaps no place at all. But wildness soon intervenes to disabuse us. The pressure of geography reasserts itself palpably and unmistakably to remind us that, of course, we could only be *here*. On the island continent the specifics are weighty and implacable. For most of the twentieth century you could have argued that amongst peoples of developed nations this felt pressure – the presence of wildness – was a default experience unique to Australians. In the richer countries the elements became inconsequential.

Feeling susceptible to the vagaries of weather was largely the lot of the poor in undeveloped places. But that was before climate change. Unpredictable and unseasonal weather has begun to erode that settled sense of immunity and now even the wealthier nations find themselves at the mercy of nature. In Europe and North America this recent vulnerability is a sudden reversal, but here it's our vivid, steady state. Climate change has intensified what we've always felt. For generations at school we sang the praises of Australia's beauty but also 'her terror'. We always knew we were subject to the whims of the wide brown land, and as extremes of weather become more commonplace this underlying perception of exposure is unlikely to fade. Nowadays bushfires don't just threaten the outskirts of timber towns, they infiltrate and ravage the suburbs of capital cities, panicking and paralyzing metropolitan populations. Flood events are no longer only the nightmare of rural riverside communities; in recent years Brisbane has been calamitously inundated. Other coastal capitals, like Perth, are so permanently drought-affected that without desalination plants they would no longer be viable settlements at all. Geography and weather have never been mere backdrop in this country, and given the obvious trends they won't be slipping from consciousness any time soon.

You only need stand on a mainland street corner in the business district and watch the desert dust fall like rain upon the gridlocked traffic to know it. Whatever else we've told ourselves, we are not yet out of nature and nature is not done with us.

Modern Australia has always been a permeable, contingent settlement and it remains so, for wherever Australians live, whether they're regional or urban, indigenous or not, there it is, pulsing and looming at any moment, like a family memory. Even out in the shimmering distance where the horizon slips and crawls implausibly in the heat, the land twitches and ticks, forever threatening to foreground itself and take over the show. The island insists, it continues to confound, enchant and appal. It fizzes, groans, creaks and roars at the perpetual edge of consciousness. For indigenous Australians this apprehension is as deep and intimate as it is ancient. It's the fruit of countless generations of experiences. For newer arrivals the feeling is fainter, inchoate, intermittent, even confused, but however tentative and vulnerable this sense of relatedness might be, it's a sign of hope. In all its range of sensitivities and perceptions, our geographically thin skin is a boon to this culture. It's good for the spirit, to be reminded as an individual or a community that there will always be something bigger, older, richer and more complex than ourselves to consider. Despite our shared successes, our mobility and adaptability, there remains an organic, material reality over which we have little control and for which we can claim no credit. To be mindful of that is to be properly awake and aware of our place.

Over great passages of time the land has always made people anew. Many of us are startled to learn how different we are from our immigrant and convict forebears, for this is a place that eventually renders people strangers to their origins. It retains a real, ongoing power to bend people out of shape, to transform them. It influences our habits and thoughts, our language, our sensory register. However stubbornly many of us might resist its influence, it moves us on somehow. In my own lifetime Australians have come to use the word 'country' as Aborigines use it, to describe what my great-great-grandparents would surely have called territory. A familial, relational term has supplanted one more objectifying and acquisitive. Over generations colonial contempt slowly and fitfully made way for diffidence. This was supplanted by an affection tempered by ambivalence and uncertainty, and in recent decades there has been an emergent admiration and respect for the land we find ourselves in. Concepts of patriotism have also evolved. A patriot need no longer devote himself to an abstraction like the state. Now a patriot will be as likely to revere the web of ecosystems that make a society possible, and a true patriot is passionate about defending this – from threats within as much as without – as if the land were kith and kin. This is why we write about it. This is why we paint it. From love and wonder, irritation and fear, hope and despair; because, like family, it refuses to be incidental.

II

Fremantle, 1999

The real estate agent shows us through the handsome Victorian house with its cricket-pitch corridors and long sash windows. It's a hot day and you can smell the sea close by.

At the rear, full of northern light, is a big room of steel

and glass into which a pond projects from outside. It's a nice touch, maybe a bit fancy for my taste, but it's water and I'm a sucker for that. I kneel a moment, expecting portly koi or some other goggle-eyed exotic, but what I see drawn up sleepily atop a slimy rock comes as such a surprise I let out an embarrassing yelp. The agent looks back. My wife comes over with that special look on her face but when she crouches beside me and peers into the pond she laughs. We're both watching a western long-necked turtle, a juvenile no larger than a child's hand.

'I knew he'd like it,' says the agent.

'You have no idea,' mutters my wife.

'There's another one hiding in there somewhere,' he says.

'Actually,' I say with great reluctance, 'the turtles could be a bit of a problem.'

'You're not turtle people, then?'

We look at each other, my wife and I. The creature stirs, unfurls its snake-like neck and clambers into the water. The good news is this is not a critically endangered swamp turtle, of which perhaps only fifty remain in the wild. Yet to keep even the more common long-necked you need a special permit, and we just know that the moment either of us asks about the paperwork for these little specimens things will get awkward.

'We're more into fish,' says my wife.

Sensing a snag, and anxious to point out the other virtues of the property, the agent bounces on the balls of his feet, but I linger at the pond, thinking of our old neighbourhood, of bare feet on yellow sand, the secretive shadowlands of reeds and tiger snakes. My wife and I grew up in adjoining streets where many yards backed onto bush and wetlands. On one side of the jarrah picket fences, parched buffalo lawns and Hills Hoists. And on the other, a wilder world of frog-song and waterbirds where kids like us ran feral. We hunted for tadpoles, gilgies, bobtails and King's skinks and did what we could to knock writhing knots of spitfires from the limbs of tuarts and marri trees. Gilgies were a prize, but of all the treasures you could come home with, the greatest trophy was the long-necked turtle.

The turtle in the pond has holed up. My wife nudges me. I haul myself upright and follow her and the agent through the rest of the house, which seems to have bought us already.

A few weeks later we take possession and as agreed the turtles are gone. I'm relieved. I could really do without the complication. But pausing at the uninhabited pond I feel a twinge of regret.

'Maybe we could stock it with gilgies,' I say.

'Maybe,' says my wife, with bigger things on her mind.

'Anything but koi,' I declare.

My wife murmurs something indistinct but vaguely affirmative.

The gilgie (*Cherax quinquecarinatus*) is a freshwater crayfish native to the streams and wetlands of south-west Western Australia. It's a hardy little creature – we learnt that as kids. A gilgie could absorb any kind of childish carelessness and swim away at day's end, and after years of drought when the swamp all but dried up they'd appear with the first rains, having burrowed into the watertable for the duration. What we didn't know as children was that gilgies are a keystone species – they play a crucial role in maintaining the health of waterways and although they're not on the brink of extinction like the western swamp turtle, their range has been severely reduced by habitat being lost to land-clearing and salination.

A week later we buy a few gilgies and I release them excitedly into the pond, but from the outset things don't go well. Our little decapods are restless and they're voting with all ten of their feet. Afterwards we realize we haven't provided enough vegetation. The pond is too clean, too clinically neat, and there's neither sufficient cover nor food. We've taken on a bunch of escape artists. At breakfast one of the kids finds a drowsy specimen under the dining table.

Another expires beside the door as if vainly awaiting its Steve McQueen moment. A third, obviously smarter, takes the outside route and makes it as far as the swimming pool, but the salt and the chlorine are his undoing.

We get koi. I lose interest in the pond. It's a sore point for many a year.

Settlers at the edge

I spent my first twelve years in the outer suburbs of Perth when the coastal bushland of Karrinyup was being bull-dozed to make way for cheap public housing. The old dunes with their ancient zamias and grasstrees were flattened. Thickets of banksia were bowled over. Groves of hardwoods like marri and tuart were razed and burnt. Churned dirt was pegged out in grids and along the new limestone tracks our outpost of progress slowly took shape. The settlement became a neighbourhood of picket fences, TV aerials and mobs of roaming kids. Homes were boxy little brick-veneer bungalows that varied only according to which side their porches faced and how fast and successfully the newcomers planted their buffalo grass and roses in the white-grey sand. Ours was at 14 Gwelup Street, on the lower side. For a long time there were no trees on our blocks, though all about us, in the no-man's-land beyond the boundaries, the bush toiled on noisily. The neighbourhood was isolated and transitional. It felt like a remote colony. Milk and bread were delivered and a couple of days a week the vegie truck crept through the streets, heralded by a jangling bell. Men drove the family car to work. There was almost no public transport. Whenever there was a vehicle free my mother and her friend next door seized on the chance to drive the few miles to the nearest butcher and from there to the hardware for heating fuel, and as my mother remembers it, 'Whoever wasn't pregnant hefted the five-gallon kero tin back to the car.' In the days before seatbelts you could squeeze five kids and a lot of shopping into a Morris Minor and it made for a ratty, rollicking trip when one bawling infant set off another, but to me these were grand excursions. When you lived in a settlement as anarchic and piecemeal as ours, six shops and a bitumen 'plaza' constituted civilization.

There was an air of promise about those early days in Gwelup Street, an unspoken sense we were making something from nothing. Everything was raw and provisional. It was like camping. Things were rough but they were *new,* and back in the 1960s newness was prized above anything else. In time, as the neighbourhood became more established, when there were no more building sites and all the fences and lawns were finally in, the looseness and excitement evaporated and a kid had to go abroad for his fun.

But in the beginning there was always the swamp at the end of the street. It was a great wild netherland that drew everything down to it eventually: water, birds, frogs, snakes – and kids of course. As we slunk off toward it, unable to resist its gravitational allure, we left the polite tinkle of sprinklers in our wake and the rowdy sounds of nature took over. We haunted the swamp and its environs barefoot. We hid in hollow logs, tried to knock parrots from trees with our gings, and in our aimless trekking we met tiger snakes, goannas, bees and strafing magpies. There were tracks through the bush everywhere and we followed them on our fat-wheeled bikes with banana seats and T-bar shifts. The swamp never ceased to enthral; it was an enig-matic place, a spot fraught with danger. The more intrepid kids in the street made rafts from the upturned roofs of old cars and paddled precariously through the reeds onto the lake. They dug deep bunkers and made humpies where they stripped stolen bikes and garnered vast collections of frogs and tadpoles and tobacco. There were stories of quicksand, of capsizes and skirmishes with strangers. Long-necked turtles scoped the surface by the shore. They dipped away like mini-subs, paddling silently out of reach of our hooked sticks. Now and then they crawled up out of the swamp and crossed the road on suicide missions, easy pickings for cars and owls and scuff-kneed kids. On the other side of the lake, market gardens pumped up the groundwater and shot it into the air as a constant halo.

At home or in school I hankered for the swamp and its thrum of life. Our street was uniform and orderly, but where it ended the chaos of another, older life resumed. Through swathes of reeds and sedges the steely surface of the lake appeared like the suddenly opened eye of God. Waterbirds rose from it in clouds. At the peaty shore everything hissed and trembled. We searched for lost tod-dlers down there, went out in phalanxes to recover dogs or bikes. We lit fires and fought them, felt the land heat and cool underfoot. Even the meekest of us went a little wild down there and we only came home when darkness fell and mothers began to bellow from every back step on the street.

Now that wildness is gone. The wetland endures but Lake Gwelup is a tidy suburban park with cycleways and gazebos. And the old neighbourhood has been smartened up. The houses we grew up in have begun to disappear. Modest bungalows are being replaced with Tuscan villas and walled compounds. My wife's childhood home still stands but number 14 was bowled over. I drive by every few years feeling a little foolish. Now it's just a place of remnants and memories, but it's long been a landscape and dream-scape in retreat. Without us ever paying much attention, the bush shrank by increments. More tuarts and marris were felled, more birds and animals displaced, more earth was scraped bare as the suburb grew and the roads around us were bitumenized. There was always fresh building activity, more families moving in, immigrants from the English Midlands, from Serbia, the Netherlands. In time the street even acquired a public phone box. People paved their drive-ways. The last big gully, a maze of tracks and bowers behind our place, was bulldozed. The trees were burnt and the ash raked flat to make way for the football oval. Year after year secret places disappeared. At the time this process felt normal and necessary, like growing up. After all, the bush was a scruffy nothing and we were civilizing it.

The biggest and most unavoidable change came when I was ten or so. Across the hill an enormous tract of bush was torn down. It seemed to happen quite suddenly. It was like a military action, with more men and machines than I'd ever seen assembled in one place. The air was black with diesel smoke as trees were battered down and rolled into windrows high as houses. For many days and nights those piles burnt like a sacked city. At sunset we rode our bikes around the perimeter to watch the sparks rise and rise into the sky. We didn't know it then but most of this land was to be sealed with asphalt. Developers built a shopping centre there the size of an airport. With all the franchises sufficient to the era, it became an ersatz indoor city. In summer its vast car parks were like baking black plains. The hyper-mall took its name from the suburb. Within a few years it was synonymous with it and in the seventies when someone spoke of 'going to Karrinyup' they generally meant the shopping centre, not the neighbourhood. On Sundays, where once we'd pedalled through the bush, pimply teenagers learnt to drive their mums' Corollas across hectares of empty, shimmering tarmac.

The land-clearing going on around us in the 1960s was

just a skirmish in a much wider assault that persists to this day. The population of Perth is growing at a hectic rate, and to accommodate the expectations of newcomers and young people wanting places of their own, the city spreads and sprawls. The bushland of the Swan coastal plain continues to be bulldozed for property developments and the urban footprint is now colossal. There's an unbroken swathe of red roof tiles from Mandurah in the south to Two Rocks, a hundred and thirty kilometres to the north. Most planners, transport gurus and environmental scientists agree that the sprawl is socially and ecologically unsustainable. Every fresh subdivision comes at the cost of bushland. And every new suburb requires infrastructure. The habitat loss from the construction of roads and freeways alone is astounding. As a result of such frenetic land-clearing the prospects of several native species of mammals, reptiles and birds look dim.

All these dwellings and suburbs are erected in a largely dry region with a shrinking rainfall pattern. But home owners still want lush lawns and European gardens, so groundwater hangs over these tracts in a perpetual reticulated mist and the waterways and aquifers absorb a steady trickle of phosphates and pesticides. From the Darling scarp to the sea the ancient, life-giving Swan River is slowly dying. Within three generations the river has gone from larder to drain. Toxic algal blooms occur summer and winter. Mass fish kills have become common in the upper reaches where black bream float belly up in their thousands and the mangroves and foreshores are spangled with their stinking carcasses. The prawns I used to catch and cook on the shore with my family every summer are gone. So too the cobbler we speared with gidgies in the shallows.

In 2009 the unique cohort of Swan River dolphins began to display mysterious lesions on their bodies and soon they were showing up like all those bream, bobbing bloated amongst the reeds and paperbarks, their hides horribly disfigured. Within a few months twenty-five percent of the dolphin population was dead. For many years, Professor Jörg Imberger, the state's most senior water researcher, has declared the river dead at depths greater than two metres. The waterway is choking on two hundred fifty-one tonnes of nitrogen every year, most of it coming from the fertilizers spread on farms and suburban lawns. First mooted in 2007, the Fertiliser Action Plan to reduce the flow of soluble phosphates into the river has yet to be implemented, and given politicians' reluctance to upset their supporters in the fertilizer industry, there seems to be no real hope it ever will be. Under pressure from recreational fishing lobbyists the state government sponsors the seasonal release of prawns, as if the waterway were a pond on a dude ranch. Meantime the emasculated Swan River Trust deploys oxygen pumps in the upper reaches and with all those busy brown bubbles the river looks and smells like a careless boy's aquarium. The Swan is desperately sick. And although a simple cure is ready to hand, the river is put on life support. Those pumps are emblematic of a city and a political culture for whom the glib fix and the photo-op will always be first choice.

I imagine there are still kids living out at the edges in transitional places like the one I knew in Karrinyup, but given the accelerated pace of change, and the ubiquity of all those surveyors' pegs, I wonder if these days they even have time enough to feel at home there.

In his memoir, *False Economy,* the nature writer William Lines describes his outdoor boyhood at Gosnells, at the other end of Perth. Brimming with bitterness and regret, he writes: 'Ever busy, ever building, ever in motion, ever discarding the old for the new, few people paused to think about what they were so busy building and what they had destroyed and thrown away. But most of what they built was depressing, brutal and ugly.'[1]

A casual excursion to the long inflamed colon of the Albany Highway between Perth and the hills will bear

Lines out. The stands of jarrah he mourns, the soaks and paddocks he remembers, have been replaced by car lots, boxy housing estates and industrial gulags. No amount of bunting is going to make any of that pretty. You have to hope some of it is worth the loss.

Like most kids I didn't imagine places had pasts. Even when I saw landforms and habitats gradually scraped away I didn't register the change for what it was. I didn't understand how permanent the forfeits would be. Humans break in order to build. And of course loss is an inevitable part of making, creating and surviving. But in exchange for what we surrender we surely have a right to expect something worthwhile, something good – developments that are mindful of their footprint, buildings that are sensitive to landscape, planning that considers the underlying cost and values change that's sustainable. Business leaders love to rhapsodize about 'a culture of excellence' but if our cities are any indication of the fruits of their labours, they seem content to bulldoze beauty and replace it with crap. The gospel of perpetual economic growth carries in its train the salvation promise of a life bigger and better for everyone. But this greater good is often mythical. The actual experiences of believers rarely bear out the claims of their faith. Even so, many adherents cleave stubbornly, fearfully to orthodoxy. I guess it's what they know. Challenging this mindset has traditionally been the work of loons, heretics and Luddites. William Lines, who identifies unashamedly with the last, writes: 'Other people must surely have found these surroundings as distressing as I did. Yet they were silent. Likely opponents lacked the vocabulary to under-stand the transformation of the world in which they lived. Few words existed to describe destruction. The dominance of the language of economics shrank alternative vocabu-laries. The leading men of Australia applauded the whole, endless clutter . . . as growth and development. With their eyes on the future, most people were too busy to notice the spreading ugliness, and they unwittingly but irrevocably bequeathed ugliness to the future.'[2]

Lots of things have changed about Perth since those days. Everything, it seems, except the attitude of those who run it, and you could say the same thing about every major city in Australia. The land speaks to so many of us, and like any long-suffering parent it yearns for a little recognition. But not everyone is paying attention.

III

Trigg Island, 1966

It's not really an island. Though it must have been one once, as the beach waxed and waned over time. For the moment it's just a huge hunk of grey-white limestone jutting into the surf. Sometimes it looks like a chunk of space rock that's come to rest on the shore. You can walk out to it along the sandspit that connects it to the beach. In its lee men launch dinghies and youths tool up with snorkelling gear to explore the reef. On the windy side, near the treacherous Blue Hole into which some luckless swimmer seems to be sucked and drowned every summer, anglers sit high above the surf on tripods casting for tailor. As waves belt in across the platform reef the fishermen are high and dry, baiting their ganged hooks with mulies and bagging fish in sacks slung from their shoulders.

The rock itself is sharp and gnarly, like the surface of an enormous, hard and pitiless meringue. It's tough to navigate but at six I know every pit and pipe, every solution hole and wind-carved cutaway, and I climb across barefoot until I find the guano-spattered shelf that obscures the gap I lower myself into.

Inside the rock it's another world. The beach noise, that white roar, is muted. There's no wind, no voices, no gulls. It's so quiet the intermittent subsea gurgles and burps sound impossibly loud and close. The tide is going out but the swell is up. I clamber down the vertical cleft to the bottom where chutes radiate landward. Here the sand underfoot is hard and wet and further in, away from the light, the jagged ceiling of the cave is damp and tawny. It smells slightly shitty in here, as if no fresh air gets in. Or maybe some kid has dropped a turd in a dark recess.

I crawl in deeper, away from the sea. Every time I come here I have the same excited, panicky sensation, and given the smell of poop, perhaps I'm not the only one. There's something fearful about being in the guts of the rock with the ocean battering outside, sluicing in through obscure vents and ducts. The atmosphere is wet and heavy. You can feel the weight of the rock hanging over you, pressing without quite touching.

Eventually I reach dry sand. The chute is low. I have to belly in with the serrated rock at my back. The light is thin and blue-grey. It's even dimmer back here where I fold up in a crescent-shaped niche, cocooned by cold stone. When I press my ear to the sand the ground hisses. It scares me. But I love the secrecy of it. At the faint sound of voices, I scoot up a narrow shaft to watch teenagers kiss in the wind and sunlight, thinking they're invisible. They have no idea I'm there.

Across the surf-wracked shelf of reef behind the couple, there are other chutes and clefts and caves – the underwater sort. I've only seen them at the lowest spring tides. If you kneel in the water you can make out the fingerlike galleries threaded with distant spots of light. In a few years, at high tide, I'll swim into them and creep my way through, angling around blind corners, watching for flutes of light up into which I spear my snorkel for a breath of air. Even then the fear isn't paramount; it's the secret place, the private space I'm seeking.

I leave the smoochers and drop back into the heart of the island. But just as I reach the sandy floor a wave thunders against the ramparts, bigger than anything all day, and in moments it rifles through the chambers, spitting, gurgling. The wind of it ruffles my hair like the approach of a train in a tunnel and instantly I'm scrambling for escape. By the time I make it to the vertical shaft the cave is awash. As whitewater wrenches at my shorts I get a handhold and scuttle up into the sun like a startled crab. The lovers barely notice me passing by.

Barefoot and unhurried

When it comes to apprehending nature kids have a significant advantage. I didn't appreciate that until I could observe my own. Now I have grandkids to reinforce the lesson as they potter about, barefoot and unhurried. You can see them taking the world in through their skin. What a blessing it is to be too young to drive, to be without a watch, to never really submit to the power of the timetable. How can you view a child's mulish refusal to wear shoes or clothes as anything but wisdom?

Being short and powerless, kids see the world low down and close up. On hands and knees, on their naked bellies, they feel it with an immediacy we can scarcely recall as adults. Remember all that wandering and dithering as you crossed the same ground again and again? It wouldn't have seemed so at the time but with all that apparently aimless mooching you were weaving a tapestry of arcane lore – where the chewy gum bulges best from the tree, where the yellow sand makes a warm pad to lie on beneath the rattling banksias – that didn't just make the world more comprehensible, but rendered it intimate, even sacred. As a kid I certainly didn't know what I was up to. But I had a feel for the blossom time of the wattle, the up-close leafiness of lichen. I knew the pong of kelp and seagrass signified the arrival of the afternoon breeze. When the southerly really got going it rattled the pods of the wild lupins and corrugated the surface of the swamp. So much is absorbed unconsciously. And now when I think of the sense memory of bindies and doublegees underfoot, and all those stubbed toes and sand-scorched soles, the splinters in the meat of the thumb, the ticks in the back of the neck and the shrivelling sting of sunburn, I grant these sensations the status of knowledge. I owe that insight to Aboriginal philosophers like David Mowaljarlai and Bill Neidjie. Whitefellas are too keen to disown the wisdom of the body, mistaking our loss of receptivity for maturity. For a while in childhood we are, as Les Murray puts it, 'all innocent authority'. Which is not to suggest we're gentle innocents. I pulled the legs off frogs to see how they worked. I robbed birds' nests and roasted ants under a magnifying glass. I harassed long-necked turtles and left tadpoles floating so long in Vegemite jars they turned into snot-monsters. I did some of it in gangs and posses. But I was happiest poking about alone.

In childhood you own little more than your secret places, the thoughts in your head. Everything else is lent to you on stern terms, so privacy and power are rare commodities. When I was a kid the house always seemed crowded. Every space, every morsel of food, every moment of quiet was contested – the shared bedroom, the tiny bathroom, the precious minutes alone in the dunny. I nurtured what privacy I had in the crooks of marri trees and burnt-out logs or in the balding hollows behind scrubby dunes. As much as I could feel it pressing on my skin, the world was growing inside my head. At times it was hard to distinguish thought from observation. In childhood such demarcation is beside the point. When I watch my infant granddaughter as she chants quietly in the mottled shade of a melaleuca and reaches for the purple-pink blossoms as if she's conjured them that very moment, I remember the fugue-like afternoons I spent staring at water, when the ripples across the shallows were private enough to be brain waves or respiration. This is when thoughts are music. So often a child's reveries spring from rhythms present in nature: the lapping rise and fall of birds stirring, settling, stirring anew; the swoon and sweep of wild oats in the wind; cicadas counting off the day in a million disapproving clicks of the tongue. It's as if we automatically tune in. I used to lie in the sun and listen to the metronomic tick of blood beneath my temples. I remember how hypnotic the stroke of my newly mastered freestyle became. There was strange comfort in the hiss of the stick I trailed in the dirt all afternoon, and in my whispery footfalls on the empty beach. Somehow it seems we rest within patterns and contours that we claim as our own but do not generate. We subside and join in effortlessly, pointlessly, never conscious we've been overcome. There's an intimacy with our surroundings we struggle to find later on in life. By the time we're grown-ups we're too busy thinking. We settle for organizing and manipulating reality, looking past ragged nature toward our intentions for it. We buy soothing soundscapes, light scented candles and join relaxation classes. We furrow our brows to study meditation. Some of us long for a bit of dreamy calm in which to nurture a secret self – no small thing in a culture suspicious of secrets and contemptuous of privacy. Once we acquire the agency of adulthood we seem to spend a hell of a lot of time seeking out the gifts and instincts of our powerless childhood. Peculiar that we should have to *learn* to relax, *strive* to let go.

It felt great, as a kid, hoarding private thoughts and secret artifacts in special places. Somehow the inkling, the site and the precious object are united in value. They are all sanctuary and sacrament; they become an enveloping, liberating field of meaning. I'm sure kids can still achieve this in high-rise apartments and McMansions – they'll always have their secrets and artifacts – but such things are easier to come by in the organic world, where a questing child, a cleft in a hidden tree, and a shell the size of a baby's ear can all be bound up in one arcane impulse.

Nowadays I live in a landscape of pindan and spinifex. Like a kid I have my trails and hollows, my secret places, my caches of pebbles and shells, my stash of arthritic-looking driftwood. I live in the littoral zone where terrestrial raptors like grey falcons cross paths with sea eagles. Getting old, you feel barefoot even in shoes. You feel the wild world anew. You're relearning things you didn't even realize you'd forgotten.

IV

Albany, 1973

Sullen, downcast and not quite thirteen, I break iron-hearted mallee roots in the afternoon gloom as a misting rain drifts in across the yard. Now and then sparks squirt and flash between the steel wedge and the nine-pound hammer. My arms ache and my elbows fizz with the impact. I hate this chore. I hate this town.

The moment I feel I've done my daily quota, I slope away without telling my mother. I head for the granites.

Like a pod of whales stranded high above the fibro neighbourhood, the dark, humpbacked monoliths are eerie, mysterious, irresistible. I cut through the peppy scrub from which this formation rises and pick my way up between calf boulders and fractured slabs. The rock surface is rough as a cat's tongue. As I climb the clash of steel on steel from the wood-chopping lingers in my fingertips and elbows. A big King's skink ravels into a fissure. Drizzle beads on the sleeves of my ugly brown school jumper. If it rains any harder I'll retreat to an overhang.

There are plenty of deep clefts in the ramparts, secret spots where staghorn lichen travels up the outer wall and where snarls of rock fig and kunzea serve as camouflage. Some days I spy older kids smoking out on a ledge or groping one another sombrely beneath the shadows of a gnarly old marlock. Today I wouldn't mind meeting someone; it'd be nice to be hailed, even challenged. But there's no one about. I don't know anyone. Half the kids in the new school just want to fight, as if blueing is fun.

I crest the biggest, highest rock as a hawk banks into an updraught and climbs away effortlessly. And there it is before me, the whole sorry town under rain, leached of colour beneath steely hills and a heavy sky. The sight of its slumped rooftops and glistening streets is deadening. I turn my back on it. Across the rock is a shallow, wide, water-filled depression, a gnamma.

I drop to my belly on the damp rock and watch insects mince across the skin of the water in the pool before me. In the end I grow bored with watching. I rest my head on folded arms and register the impossible mass of stone beneath me. It begins to feel warm, like a sleeping beast that might stir.

Disgust and enchantment

When I was twelve my family left the suburbs of Perth and moved south to Albany. It was a radical dislocation. For a long time I was lonely and miserable and from the outset it seemed that the weather and the landscape of this new environment were conspiring to make things worse. Gone were the blue skies, the bright tutting of cicadas, the roasting consolation of the sun. I missed my friends, but I also felt the loss of home territory – the soughing dune sheoaks and dusty limestone scales of the dry sand country of the midwest. Here in the south a gothic gloom hung over the landscape. There were actual mountains in the distance. Sometimes snow whitened their peaks. Albany cowered between high rainswept tors, and the wind-torn harbour was flecked like the lips of a lunatic. Just as the local kids seemed to seethe and spoil for a bit of biff at school, the town felt like it was always about to lash out. It was dark, tamped down, sodden, but hot and unpredictable underneath, like a peaty paddock.

Out of town the hilly, crenellated coast was covered by olive-silver heath growing so low and spare it looked alpine. Gloomy black extrusions of granite reared from the scrub and on the high ridges above the sea their moody, chiselled faces shone like gods in the brief flashes of sun between squalls. The rain misted, pelted, dripped and stung. Inland, dark aggregations of red tingle and karri laboured against a sky as grey and cheerless as a sodden army blanket. The crowns of those giant trees were torn by gales and yet at ground level they didn't move. The vegetation smelt odd. Beneath the karri trees the understorey stank like cat piss.

The hakeas reeked of human poop and everything else smelled like some maiden aunt's tea-tree-oil furniture polish. The leaf litter was deep, soft and slimy. Lurid funguses and squelching mops of moss clung to trunks and branches. So much of the bush was wet and dark. There seemed to be no flowers at all. Like the amateur botanist Georgiana Molloy a century and a half before me, I was bewildered and intimidated by what she called these 'sombre eucalypts'. They were majestic in their way but en masse they were indeed opaque and eerie in their 'unbounded limits of thickly clothed dark green'.[3]

It was a surprise to be afraid of the bush, but I'd never encountered this kind of scale and colour palette before. A tree the width of a car is impressive. Thousands of them together are a little unnerving; they press at you, cause your spirit to retract until you feel about as consequential as a beetle.

But in spring I saw flowers – callistemons, wattles, orchids. There were things I'd been brushing past that I didn't even know were blossoms. After a gale, drifts of white from the blooming peppermints frosted the dirt. Bloody petals of red flowering gums dotted the coast. In the gullies the stately musk of boronia (including a species bearing Molloy's name) rose like the smell of a country dance. At night trippy, luminescent mosses glowed milky green in clumps and the bush smelt crisp, clean, strong.

We were only in Albany three years. So I still puzzle over the disproportionate impact the place had on me. I think of the experience as a chain of sensory assaults. Or maybe it's fairer to call them epiphanies of disgust. In its way the town itself seemed rather genteel. With its old Victorian cottages and churches it looked English. The preponderance of retired farmers and impossibly staid townies rendered sections of the place peaceable, conservative and dowdy, but along the waterfront there was another civic reality entirely, for here lay the wildness beneath the veneer. Down from the rugged, racist pubs of the terrace, the jetties and wharves were a literal connection to the primal savagery that had animated the place since colonization. At the docks every afternoon the tuna men came alongside beneath a shitting cloud of gulls. Nearby deckhands hosed gore from the whale-chasers at their moorings. Further along, the shift-horns of the factories bawled and greasy steam billowed across the railway tracks. Those great work barns, the fish cannery, the abattoir, the wool mill and the superphosphate factory, chugged and roared day and night, every one of them spewing effluent into the harbour. It honked down there. The estuarine shallows were livid with algal blooms and ramparts of toxic slime mounted around the shore. The water's edge, you quickly understood, was bloody, dirty and dangerous. But this was what the town was built on: a century and a half of seizing, killing, breaking and boiling.

In time I saw a lot of this savagery firsthand, the sperm whales dragged flukes first up the flensing deck, their heads hacked off with a steam-powered saw. The sharks shot and clubbed. The beef carcasses sliding by like dry-cleaned coats on endless racks. The viscous blood hosed across the concrete. I stood on beaches as biblical draughts of salmon were hauled ashore in nets and shovelled onto tip-trucks, leaking crimson on the sugar-white sand. Those tonnes of salmon were carted off for pet food.

A copper's son, I sniffed the reeking desperation of the lockup, saw the squalor of the native reserve. I witnessed sudden, vicious fights, steered around drunks sleeping in puddles of their own piss and saw bullet holes in car doors. I overheard the whispered accounts of rape and suicide and slowly put the stories and names and faces together. For the best part of a year I saw only dark, unknowable nature and brutal humanity and I felt lost.

In time it was the long and lonely coast that lifted my spirits. The white southern beaches won me over. They were the purest, the least trammelled and the loveliest I'd ever seen. And there were so many of them. Every granite headland hid a new cove, another rivermouth, a grove of tea-trees, an empty camping spot, a beachbreak where the water was turquoise and the waves unridden. The low skies and grim hills and misted cliffs began to seem wild and grand. Perhaps it was because I was now seeing them from the water where I spent every hour of freedom I could beg, borrow or burgle. Surfing was not just my escape, it was my way into a place that had previously felt as if it were resisting me. This was the beginning of my lifelong love of the southern coast and its hinterland.

It's easy to imagine surfing as mere sensation, mindless vigour; narcotic, repetitive activity. It's certainly that. But for me it was never only that. Because for all those hectic moments spent hurtling across the water (or bouncing along the seabed in a welter of sand and foam) there are hours more spent bobbing on the surface. This is when a surfer does little else but watch and wait. The watching and waiting are the bulk of what it means to be out surfing. It's about observation as much as anticipation. In adolescence I was hooked on the creaturely thrills of momentum and submission. Half of a young man's rebelliousness is the quest for a worthy force, something large to submit to. Hence the flirting with danger, the often disastrous compulsions and addictions. For me, the secret release of surfing was the experience of being overtaken. Flying across a breaking swell, I loved the giddy speed, but what I needed most was the feeling of being monstered by a force beyond my control. This was how I came to understand nature and landscape. By submitting. And by waiting.

Waiting sharpens the senses. Which is to say it erodes preconceptions and mutes a certain kind of mental static; the clutter and glare in the foreground recede. Immersion and duration are clarifying. While waiting for the next set, for the wind to change, or the tide to turn, I had thousands of hours in which to notice things around me. I began to put them together geographically. Beaches, for instance, were constantly subject to dynamic processes. In fact a seashore, now I saw it clearly, was a live system. And so was a creek, a coastal heath, a forest. Even a blunt dolerite cliff was somehow in motion, under power, subject to endless force. Forefront and backdrop, wave and shore, tree and stone, it was all network and linkage. Some of it was obviously beautiful – the blue-green water, the sparks given off by chalky white sand when you chuffed your feet through it – but the beauty of other things lay in how they worked, how they caused stuff to happen elsewhere. The way a storm in the Antarctic produced an echo that became a completely distinct event in my own world. From some unspeakable terror across the horizon came a day of pleasure for me. Surf was old energy transformed. And so were granite monoliths or karri trees. Everything I saw was an unfinished and perpetually open-ended process. In its mass and in its physical arrangement, the bush bore the consequences of occurrences unwitnessed and unrecorded.

At thirteen or fourteen I had only the fuzziest apprehension of the natural world, but this is where my reverence for it began. This growing awareness had a mystical tinge to it, it's true, but by and large its inspiration was material, the result of long immersion in the physical facts. In my case it was a very literal suspension and absorption, for when you're in the water all day, day upon day, with dolphins and sea lions, when you swim in a shoal of salmon beneath a halo of diving birds, it's hard for even the most dull-witted boy to ignore the inkling that you're a small part of a larger process.

But I was a boy of my time, the son of a culture still resisting such notions as submission to a greater complexity. In the seventies Australians were devoted uncritically to the conquest and mastery of nature. The only encouragement I had in thinking of the world in more relational terms was from the weathered old hippies I occasionally bummed rides home with. They had an undisguised awe for the ocean and whimsical, Aquarian notions about ecology. They were dreamy, dope-addled loafers but I enjoyed hearing their muddled disquisitions about how the 'straight' culture had lost its way. I guess their outlook was mostly hedonistic romance. They lived off the taxpayer and produced nothing you could hold in your hands. Their kids were snot-nosed and the women looked ancient and careworn. People at church said they were degenerates, but in a town where butchering whales and poisoning the harbour were respectable activities, that didn't count for much.

I fell in love with the south. I hiked and camped along the coast, fished for groper from rockshelves, dived for abalone, climbed in the Stirling Range and trekked in the Porongurups. These places, the mountains and rivers, headlands and beaches, ate into me, scoring me for life.

Inhuman scale introduced me to process and to earthly mystery in a way that school largely failed to. It taught humility out of season. It drew upon the wonder I had as a child but was pressured to disown as an adolescent. This is a tough time to be humbled because you already feel reduced and traduced at every turn; you're utterly resistant, fending away for dear life. Yet when I felt tiny in nature I became calm, the rage dissipated. Somehow it was better to be bounced and flogged across the seabed, subjugated by the impersonal ocean, than to be singled out for humiliation in company. It was a relief to be dominated by something without malice.

I've been drawing on such experiences for decades; those landscapes are the bedrock of my stories and novels and they draw me back, haunt me, feed me still.

Whenever I return to the south-west I am of course reminded of adolescence, of people I knew and things I did, but the surge of feeling that overtakes me isn't nostalgia so much as recognition, a kind of sense memory that has never diminished. No matter how long I've been away this sensual familiarity means I quickly have my bearings. The wind off the happily rehabilitated harbour. Faint sun glancing from granite tors. Just a whiff of peppery coastal heath or a glimpse of the bloody blossoms of flowering gums and I'm confident. The ground feels firm beneath my feet. I don't live there anymore but it still feels like home.

V

Cape Keraudren, 1997

Headed for Broome in September, I pull over early one afternoon to camp for the night at the southern end of Eighty Mile Beach. Once I've gathered driftwood and unrolled my swag on the white sand, I blow an hour casting lures to the incoming tide. Just before dark I get a savage strike and the reel fizzes and whines as something big takes off across the flats. After a few minutes of exertion and excitement I have it bucking, wild and silver in the shallows at my feet, and when I grab the leader and swim the furious thing ashore I find I've landed a fish I've never seen before. Chrome-sleek, as thick and long as my arm, it sports rows of nasty, curving fangs every bit as sharp as they look. While I struggle to set it free it flails and lashes. Within a few moments it's gone in a blur and I'm left, startled and bleeding, coated in the sort of mucus you'd only expect to encounter in a science-fiction movie.

Back at camp, despite the adhesive slime that glues my fingers together and turns my fish identification book into an expensive papier-mâché fan, I see I have met my first wolf herring. I spend half the hot night scraping the fish's ectoplasmic smegma from my hands and shins.

In the morning the sheet is grafted to my hairy legs and my fingers are webbed. I get the sense the wolf herring has had the last laugh.

I walk the flats at low tide. The first rays of sun sting my bare back. The outfalling sea has left a vast, ribbed field of sandy pools and rivulets like an abandoned kingdom. But up close the thin strips of water are busy with crabs and fingerlings, spider stars, bivalves. I stalk from one silvery fractal to the next between the wallows of skippers, the sandballs of ghost crabs and the mud-poots of worms. It's a long, bare stretch of beach and it looks lifeless but the whole place pops and sighs and rattles. Everywhere there's evidence of life, seen and unseen. I forget the indignity of the wolf herring. The morning feels like a gift.

I really should hit the road – there's another long day of driving ahead – but the sea at the horizon is milky blue and the puddles are warm. I meander on without a soul in sight.

At a rocky pool I catch a flicker of movement and spy a blenny wriggling about feverishly, searching for a crack or a bit of loose sand for cover. I stand quite still but whatever I do the goofy little critter charges around in a panic.

Then I see the bright shell at the far end of the pool. It's like a half-buried cowrie, brilliant with splashes of purple and yellow-brown and blue, and in this tawny sandscape the colours are extravagant; it looks ravishing. As I stoop to reach for it all the colours swim before me; they seem to reconstitute themselves and the blue dots become livid, engorged. The effect causes me to hesitate, disoriented. My hand hovers above the water. And then my brain catches up. Those swirling blue rings, the sudden swelling mass. That's not a shell – it's a blue-ringed octopus. The tiny creature's main weapon is a neurotoxin twelve hundred times stronger than cyanide. Pick that up and I'd be dead before I reached the vehicle.

I straighten with a start. I don't even pause to rescue the blenny. I abandon him to his fate.

The corner of the eye

I was always curious. As a kid I was a lurker and an eaves-dropper. Sometimes I'd poke at things with sticks to see what they did – anemones, skinks, roadkill. But mostly I was content to watch.

Like any kid I was told not to stare. But I stared all the

time – and at the oddest things. I found if you gazed hard enough at a handful of sand the individual grains became enormous; you could see cavernous spaces between them. There was so much air between particles you were surprised dirt weighed anything at all, and when you tipped it free the hiss it made as it fell to earth was like the sound of all that air escaping. When you looked at things long enough your gaze seemed to alter what you were looking at. It felt like a quirk of optics, a sleepy trick.

But young or old, stare as we might, much of what we learn about the objects of our attention in the natural world seems to come from out of the corner of the eye. When you're not trying to dig a place up with your eyes, a feeling for what's present will creep up on you, seep into vision and consciousness. Sometimes seeing is about duration and experience. This is the hard lesson newcomers have had to learn here on this continent. When Dutch mariners began making landfall in the early seventeenth century they were confounded by what they saw. Almost two centuries later the French and English similarly viewed the enigmatic southland through the lens of their own hemisphere. And they were appalled. *Terra australis* didn't correspond to what they expected or understood; it wasn't simply that they were baffled by the land and its indigenes – what they saw offended them. It seemed deranged and perverse. To the English buccaneer William Dampier, who visited the north-west coast in 1688 and 1699, the new land was a kingdom of sand and flies. True, he'd landed in a particularly tough bit of country around Shark Bay, but his disgust obscured and distorted what and who stood before him. And for Dampier the flies became an obsession. As he saw it the indigenes were 'the most miserable wretches in the universe', and the root cause of their apparently degraded state was the tyranny of flies, because 'from their infancy being thus annoyed with these insects, they do never open their eyes as other people: and thus they cannot see far'. The irony of this misperception is bittersweet, but in the annals of exploration it's hardly an exception. Europeans came to these shores fired by a spirit of adventure and acquisitive curiosity and they often left sorely disheartened. The intensity of their revulsion and dismay lingers in place names all over Australia, and there's no shortage of examples here in the west – Useless Loop and Lake Disappointment, just for starters.

But the expeditioners' reports weren't always so downbeat. Later champions of empire saw what was expedient; they were eager to please their betters back home. And some, like James Stirling, found ways of seeing that neatly aligned imperial imperatives with their own ambitions. Before Stirling had even visited the Swan River region, which he did in 1827, he was sold on it. He had a picture in his mind already. The French maps he'd studied convinced him it was the perfect spot for a strategic colonial outpost and when he finally laid eyes on the place his enthusiasm was undimmed. To the nabobs at home he praised it in terms lavish enough to cause a modern local to blush. Perhaps he really did see the region this way. For somehow he saw things the French navigator Jules Dumont d'Urville hadn't. In fact he saw virtues he needed to see, things that simply weren't there. The excellent anchorages, plentiful water, fertile soils and teeming game of his reports were fabrications that cost many unsuspecting settlers their fortunes and their lives. And thus was born a grand West Australian tradition. Land scams, sharp practice and large-scale fraud have been distinguishing features of the state's history ever since. The twin tendencies so integral to the settlement of the Swan River region, the ability to see what is plainly not there and a studious failure to notice what is, are deeply ingrained in local culture and politics.

Nineteenth-century explorers locked the land into the grids of their imperial maps. Creatures of their time, they ignored features or beings superfluous to their vision. Many were geographers and naturalists, men of the Enlightenment, trained to observe and record, but there was a lot of the continent they simply could not see for looking and this problem persisted well into the next century. Travelling in Australia between the wars, and living for a time in the hills east of Perth, D.H. Lawrence struggled doggedly to see past the limits of his cultural understanding. He was an exceptionally sensitive observer, but when he tried to apprehend the mysterious bush it evaded and confounded him. 'You feel you can't *see*,' he wrote in *Kangaroo*, 'as if your eyes hadn't the vision in them to correspond with the outside landscape.'[4]

Eventually – and very slowly – experience gave newcomers and their native-born children fresh means of seeing and reading landforms. The extent to which Aborigines shared lore and traded information is often overlooked, as is the curiosity and openness they frequently displayed in early encounters. Many acts of kindness spared the lives of shipwrecked Europeans. In 1875 survivors of the *Stefano*, which foundered on the coral shoals of Ningaloo Reef, were aided and protected by a band of Aborigines. After four months of patient guidance and steady walking through some of the harshest country imaginable, the last of them, Michael Baccic and Ivan Juric, were calmly delivered to the cutter

Jessy, anchored in the lee of the North West Cape.

Much earlier than this the diplomacy, curiosity and fellow-feeling of clans and individuals along the south coast prevented the deaths of many English settlers and soldiers, even securing the survival of whole settlements, and there's no better example of this than the Minang warrior of the Noongar people, Mokare, who distinguished himself at King George's Sound, the military encampment that eventually became Albany. He was a man of rare wit, adaptability and generosity who did what he could to draw the clumsy invaders into a relationship of mutual respect, earning the affection of influential colonists who recognized his largeness of spirit and relied upon him. A teacher as much as a guide, he was a visionary in his way, pivotal in creating and maintaining the amity and co-operative spirit of the so-called 'friendly frontier' at a time when successive commandants of the garrison afforded native custom and hunting grounds the sort of respect that was hardly typical in the colonial era. Mokare formed abiding relationships with newcomers, especially those like resident magistrate Alexander Collie whose curiosity and openness was almost a match for that of the Noongar statesman. Mokare died in 1831. Four years later the magistrate was buried beside his friend, as he'd requested.

But Mokare's dream of ongoing reciprocity between Aborigines and settlers died with him. In Albany the wisdom of indigenes was soon disregarded, and as the settlers consolidated their position their attitudes hardened. Useful and even vital advice offered them was either ignored, ridiculed or taken for granted. In a land where climatic and seasonal conditions were radically different to those of the Northern Hemisphere such information could be critically important to the newcomers' survival. In those all too rare instances when the interlopers actually understood the value of Aboriginal counsel, which after all drew upon the research and development of countless generations, they gave nothing in return. Just as they'd come to seize land and game and access by main force, they grabbed information without a thought for notions of exchange, establishing a sorry pattern of ignorance and contempt that endured well into the next century, to the great and lasting cost of millions of Australians, black and white.

All over the continent in the nineteenth century, as colonists began to attain a familiarity that wasn't quite commensurate with their territorial gains, disdain for the first peoples and a suspicion of the 'fickleness' and 'treachery' of the new lands created a sort of siege mentality. Relations with indigenes became increasingly high-handed and martial, and even where clans were routed and 'dispersed' by massacres, the rather wild-eyed, aggro-defensive mindset endured. For the bulk of our history since 1788 Australians' attitude to the land has been almost exclusively warlike. Every gold rush was a pillaging skirmish, a raid for booty, and for most miners the engagement was brief, brutal and fruitless. In the wake of each frenzied campaign the land lay gouged and despoiled for decades, even centuries, and few retreating combatants ever spared the places they'd ruined another thought. And while it's fair to say generations of farming and grazing produced a closer feeling to country, even an intimacy of sorts, agriculturalists have engaged in a long action of subjugation from which they are yet to fully relent. The love they claim to have for the land is sometimes more a reflection of the work they and their families have invested in it, and when they declare that love, often what they really mean is they're wedded to the lifestyle. And we don't talk about it much, but there is another kind of fellow feeling – the tender spot we have for the vanquished opponent. There's nothing like the sentimental soft focus we grant someone or something that's no longer a threat. Still, I think attitudes really have changed, and the emotions many farmers express when talking about country are deeper, more intense and far less martial than those of their forebears.

I guess we learn to love by experience. Despite it, too. True, some fondness is bought, especially on the frontier. Many fortunes were quickly made in the nineteenth century, in wool, wheat and gold. A century later people got rich from property speculation and iron ore – and what's not to love about a place that makes you quickly and unthinkably rich? Most folk, though, have had to come to a more gradual accommodation with their environs. As migrants they only liked what they knew, but over time Australia *was* what they knew, and for their children it was all they knew. However else it was viewed in the Old World, they'd come to think of this country as theirs. And eventually, in the 1940s when a Japanese invasion seemed imminent, they were forced to defend it as their home. Until that point, only the continent's first peoples had ever truly fought for their country.

For all these disparate and largely incidental reasons, our attitude to the landscape and the species it supports has changed. The fragility of ecosystems and the consequences of the old frontier ethic have impressed themselves upon scientists and farmers alike, and land is slowly beginning to be used more sensitively. Land-clearing practices are much more strictly monitored and even the most rapacious of miners are required to address the non-monetized values of the country they want to dig, and submit to the regime of environmental assessment they complain of as 'green tape'.

The gradual transformation from a combative to a more cordial inclination has not just been a matter of attrition. A lot of it is the fruit of inspiration. All through Australia's brief modern history, before the compounding experience of generations helped wear people into different shapes and rendered them open to country in ways that were alien to their ancestors, there were always outriders and eccentrics who saw beyond the bounds of their European inheritance. Some newcomers responded immediately and instinctively to Australia. They approached its unutterable strangeness with curiosity and delight. Every Australian community and era had its share of amateur botanists, its Sunday painters, moony middle sons and lonely wives for whom the ranges, gullies, saltpans and forests need be no more useful than music, no more in want of mastery than birdsong. From colonial times to the digital age there have been poets, songsters and nature mystics, bushwalkers, birdwatchers and enlightened farmers for whom the land is first and foremost a source of wonder. Many of them had the good fortune to meet and learn from Aborigines whose pride in the wisdom of their own cultures and whose reverence for country endured. With the aid of this counsel and their own experience, native-born Australians without indigenous heritage came to the realization that the natural world – even this peculiarly misunderstood tranche of it – has intrinsic value. But theirs has been the dissenting tradition; these were our conscientious objectors to the war on nature. In my own lifetime this cryptic cultural thread has emerged into the open to become a social movement. But when I was a kid such thinking was novel indeed.

My first exposure to a more considered view of nature was probably through Vincent Serventy (1916–2007). The youngest of eight children to Croatian immigrants and brother to the eminent ornithologist Dominic Serventy, he wrote or co-wrote more than seventy books. Growing up in the hills overlooking Perth and 'running wild through the bush like a brumby', as he put it, he became a teacher and filmmaker and was far and away the most prominent naturalist and conservation campaigner of his time. His environmental outlook was prophetic and his passion for communicating it to a lay audience was indefatigable. Many years before the appearance of Harry Butler, who was a former student, and the 'crocodile hunter' Steve Irwin, who was an unconscious but very successful imitator, Serventy was there, giving public lectures, making documentaries, using the new medium of television to expose natural history to ordinary punters. Few Australians ever did more to excite and educate their countrymen about their environment. His 1966 *Nature Walkabout* was our first homegrown TV nature show and I wasn't the only Australian to be mesmerized by the excursions he led into the remote interior. He often took artists along to immerse them in wild landscapes and the fruits of his evangelizing impulse are plain to see in the sketches and paintings of Frank Hodgkinson, Tim Storrier and especially John Olsen, who continued to paint Lake Eyre obsessively and reverentially for decades after Serventy took him to see it in flood in the 1970s.

Lake Eyre, or Kati Thanda, is fifteen metres below sea level, the continent's lowest point. When I was a kid it was only notable as a racetrack, the proving ground of Donald Campbell's pursuit of the land speed record in his gas-powered *Bluebird*. To the untrained observer it's little more than a vast saltpan, but on the rare occasions it fills, when the rivers of three states literally run 'backwards', it reveals its hidden life in an efflorescence so remarkable as to be regularly described as miraculous. For a few months it becomes one of the largest lakes in the world. Millions of bony herring and golden perch seem to erupt from the desert sands and billions of birds descend upon it from all over the world. Having seen the desert transformed in 1974 Olsen came to think of landscape 'as a nervous system', as if he'd gotten past surfaces and gone deeper. He never quite shook this place and these events off. Previously steeped in European ways of seeing, Olsen was one of the first non-indigenous painters to sense in this country an organic whole, a web of interdependent relationships, and Vin Serventy deserves some credit for that.

Years before the Lake Eyre expedition, Serventy took Perth's most famous son, Rolf Harris, on a 'safari' from Darwin into the red centre to make a TV series called *Rolf's Walkabout*. It was an early example of a filmmaker using a celebrity to reach a popular audience. With its canny mix of outback adventure and nature documentary, the show followed the meandering progress of the Harris and Serventy families as they juddered down red dirt tracks, camped in creekbeds and came upon all manner of creatures and landscapes, and though very much a product of its time, with the popular entertainer always front and centre, it was shaped by Serventy's pedagogical imperative, and it introduced many suburban Australians like myself to the wonders and fragility of the ecology of our homeland. I was entranced by every episode. The families featured were famous, but the Harris and Serventy kids were about my age; I could instantly see myself in their place, parting reeds to spy on freshwater crocs in billabongs, turning over desert rocks to find thorny devils, chasing goannas through the spinifex. In 1971, when Carol Serventy and Alwen Harris published a spin-off in the wake of the show, Mum gave it to me for Christmas and I treasured that book above all others. In retrospect it's a gauche production, particularly in its desultory and picturesque portrayal of Aboriginal lives and cultures, but what most affected me at the age of eleven was that the ecology, usually relegated to mere backdrop in Australian stories and TV shows, was suddenly the focus – vast flocks of wild budgerigars, eerie fields of termite mounds, wetlands and savannahs teeming with life. Instead of stuff to look past to the story at hand, these things *were* the story at hand. Thanks to *Rolf's Walkabout* I learnt about quolls, plumed pigeons, jabirus and pandanus palms. It was my first exposure to Aboriginal cave painting. More than a tantalizing entrée into the remote interior, it quickened my interest in the plants and creatures closer to home and in a real sense it taught me to pay attention, to see beyond the initial glance. The book and TV series were influential in other ways, too, because when I was a kid the accepted wisdom was that nothing of significance came out of Perth or Western Australia. Of course in those days the old cultural cringe held sway for many Australians, but in the west we had our own thing going, a continental cringe that was especially crippling and self-defeating, so as a boy it was unutterably exciting to see people from my hometown on television and in the printed pages of a book. There they were, people from Bassendean, Bickley, Subiaco embarking on intrepid adventures, witnessing marvels of nature that were the envy of the world.

I've only held onto a handful of books from my childhood. *Rolf's Walkabout* is one of those. Not even Harris's late disgrace could convince me to give it up. I keep it out of nostalgia. Also to honour Vin Serventy, whose passion lit something in me that never died. To my mind it'll always be *Vin's Walkabout*. Rolf was just the beard. When I pull the book down from the shelf to check it against my memories, it falls open naturally to page 27. And there is a photo of Serventy's daughter Cathy. Holding a long-necked freshwater turtle.

For more than half a century, from Dryandra to Lake Pedder, Serventy seemed to leave his fingerprints on almost every attempt to save wild Australia from destruction. In the mid-sixties he joined forces with that other heretic, Judith Wright, with whom he embarked upon the long and bitter struggle to spare the Great Barrier Reef from a fate as a limestone mine. Figures like these and their early collaborator, Eddie Hegerl, then a young marine scientist, were seen as kooks and troublemakers for daring to suggest that the reef had value beyond the profits it might yield as a quarry. For the politicians and their clients in the business community of Queensland, such crusaders were a new obstacle to negotiate. At the outset their views about natural heritage were too outlandish to be taken seriously. These nutters simply didn't understand the facts of life. Of course corals were pretty in their way, if you fancied that sort of thing, but like all facets of nature they were there to be exploited. This was the obvious order of things, so there was no fear of febrile and slightly effeminate notions like 'intrinsic value' and 'ecological fragility' infecting the minds of the young and impressionable. But the defenders of the reef refused to go away. This was when things really got nasty. Eddie Hegerl and his comrades were pilloried, defamed and menaced by the corrupt Bjelke-Petersen government. Reviled as they were by the burghers of Brisbane, the dissenters would not be dismissed, and to the great surprise of the establishment their view of the reef held sway. Years of dogged advocacy led to it being declared a marine park and finally accorded World Heritage status. Nowadays the reef is Australia's most prized and visited natural asset. It's one site that probably even deserves the 'iconic' status that's so biliously overused in tourism bumf and infotainment. The place is sacred for any number of reasons, not least of which is that it's the locus of a seminal turning point in our culture. The first major battleground upon which the conscientious objectors took the colours. Fifty years on, the eccentric outlook of the 'ratbags' who made it possible is more or less mainstream.

But despite this, in the past thirty years coral cover has diminished by half. The reef is assailed every day by fishing pressure, toxic runoff from agriculture and coastal development, increased shipping movement, and the sedimentation associated with dredging. As if these weren't threats enough to a system vulnerable to climate change, the federal government has been keen to exploit the world's largest coal deposit in the Galilee Basin, and to dig seven new deepwater ports for coal terminals along the shores of the Great Barrier Reef Marine Park. It was no surprise to hear scientists and tourism operators express concerns about the effect of millions of cubic metres of dredge spoil and massive plumes of sediment on the corals' health, but it was startling to have a Queensland premier counter with the assertion that Australia was, after all, 'in the coal business'. The prime minister, Tony Abbott, was even more dismissive. 'Coal,' he said, 'is good for humanity.' Utterances like these roused an entirely new generation to leap to the defence of the reef, and after many months of pressure, and critical scrutiny by UNESCO, the government staged a blustering retreat. The future of the reef is by no means secure, but there's hope in the fact that public consensus about its value has neither waned over time nor been undermined by the best efforts of the fossil fuel lobby and their friends in government.

In the 1970s environmentalists, as they'd come to be called, were still embattled outliers, but as a schoolboy in Albany, the last whaling town in Australia, I felt the first inklings of their disruptive and chaotic potential. Years before activists put an end to the industry in 1978 their ideas were slowly taking root in our community, where the legitimacy of whaling had rarely been questioned. At fourteen I was disturbed to discover that the sperm whales and humpbacks targeted by our local enterprise were on the verge of extinction. Overnight the ritual excursion to the Frenchman Bay whaling station to scoff and roar as tourists puked from the lookout above the flensing deck felt moronic. All this carnage and waste for fertilizer and cosmetics. What had always seemed normal was suddenly as absurd and reckless as it was grotesque, but to say so in Albany where whalers enjoyed a special reputation, an afterglow of colo-nial romance, was to risk alienation. I remember the look of shock and anger on the company manager's face when I con-fronted him in an interview for the local radio station that began as an English assignment and got a little out of hand. In the early seventies a local burgher in a country town like ours wasn't often challenged in any forum, let alone on air. Here was the representative of a venerated industry faced with a fourteen-year-old upstart who thought the best way to get to the bottom of things was to keep asking 'Why?' He survived my dry-mouthed and inarticulate grilling well enough but before long – and entirely without my help, I might add – the community was polarized on the matter. There were suddenly more and far smarter people asking questions, wondering why the industry persisted given the whales' perilous status. Anyone who expressed reservations about it was deemed to have fallen prey to the influence of outsiders and big-city troublemakers. At high school the wrong word at an inopportune moment could earn you a smack in the chops.

The debate took a few years to come to a head. By the time the 'greenies' came to town in force I'd moved away. In my first year of university, I followed the news from Perth. Day after day the protesters dogged the whale chasers in tiny

inflatables, putting themselves between the explosive har-
poons and the whales. They were brave people, foolhardy,
really, and they had the good fortune to find themselves
pitted against mariners of great skill and decency, without which some campaigners may well have died. One of
the first Australian environmental struggles to feature this
sort of high-stakes direct action, it was in its way a seminal
campaign, but it was also clumsy and needlessly divisive.
I was troubled by the high-handedness of some protesters.
There was a contempt for working people in general, and
country folk in particular, that disgusted me. The inclusive,
democratic impulses of visionaries like Judith Wright and
Vin Serventy were too often subsumed by something cultic
and exclusionary, and the memory of these excesses helped
temper my work as an activist later in life.

In the 1980s 'greenie' subculture began to broaden and
become a social movement, though it was still fractious
and hectic. With its unlikely national reach and surprising
political consequences, Tasmania's Franklin Dam blockade
was evidence of how widely the thinking of those earlier
prophetic figures had spread, and how potent it was when
amplified by a new and more diverse generation of activists
like Bob Brown. By the 1990s the erudition, discipline and
strategic patience of advocacy groups meant that ideas once

thought to be harmlessly eccentric were shaping the vernacular mood and framing public policy. And by the turn of the millennium the status of a river, reef or forest could determine the outcome of an election. A forest campaign swept Geoff Gallop to power in Western Australia in 2001. Back then commentators suggested this might be an aberration, a one-off, but in 2015 Campbell Newman's cavalier stewardship of the Great Barrier Reef was instrumental in him losing power in Queensland.

While I was always passionate about nature, I never saw myself as an ecowarrior. In fact I avoided joining environmental organizations, even when my children were members in their primary school years. Still, by the early 1990s I was conscious of a diminution in the ecosystems I knew best, the limestone reefs and islets of the midwest coast. Wherever I swam in a mask and snorkel I was seeing more and more of less and less. Coastal development and fishing pressures were having an unmistakable impact. When I was a kid abalone encrusted every shoreline shelf and surf-washed crag. They were so plentiful we baited our lobster pots with them. Nowadays they're scarce and under immense fishing pressure. As a result the abalone season in Western Australia is five hours long. That's five hours a year.

In the end I felt I couldn't avoid being involved in environmental matters. The natural world has always been my prime inspiration. I felt indebted. Soon after I became formally engaged in marine conservation, I got an unexpected letter from Vin Serventy. He was in his late seventies and still working like a man half his age. I had him and that letter in mind years later when I reluctantly became the public face of a campaign to save Australia's second great coral reef. Vin didn't hector. He had the great teacher's gift of drawing people in and getting them interested in something about which they knew very little, and he sought to build bridges and harness goodwill. He died in 2007. I never met him. But whether helping defend sharks and turtles, or advocating for a national system of marine parks, I've tried, as a layman, to follow in his train.

I was thirty-one and a father of three before I got to swim with a whale shark. As a kid I'd seen Hans Hass and Cousteau diving with these massive creatures in documentaries, but I never thought I'd get the chance until George King, a crusty rogue from Exmouth, took me out to Ningaloo Reef on his lovely old boat the *Nor-Don*. I assumed we were going to see some coral and maybe catch a tuna, but just beyond the breakers, in fifty metres of water, George pulled the engine out of gear, told me to get my mask and fins on and jump into the water without delay. I went over the side in my undies and came face to face with a creature the size of a small submarine. It was one of the most unexpected thrills of my life. I felt overcome by the reef, claimed by it.

George was no greenie rabble-rouser. He was a legendary spearfisherman who made his living as a charter boat operator and publican. But he was passionate about whale sharks. He pioneered the ecotourism industry based upon them that's now famous the world over. I think the old bugger knew exactly what he was doing when he pitched me over the side.

Ningaloo is the continent's largest fringing coral reef. Unlike the Great Barrier Reef, it's close to shore. At certain points you can literally wade out into it to see turtles, black-tipped sharks, dugongs, lagoon rays, and dozens of species of coral. From a boat in a single morning – sometimes within an hour – you can swim with an eight-metre whale shark, a fleet of manta rays, and more fish than you can name, all within sight of the red desert ranges that rise from behind its beaches. Heading back to the lagoon you'll usually see humpbacks, hyperactive schools of Spanish mackerel, and even orcas. But being so close to shore the reef is especially vulnerable to fishing pressures and coastal development. Since 1987 a developer had been trying to build a luxury marina resort right in the beating heart of the place. Successive governments were supportive and key media outlets openly barracked for the project. At the turn of the millennium the momentum for it looked unstoppable. But a handful of activists and organizers had other ideas. With pitifully modest resources they mounted a campaign to defend the reef. When I became the public face of Save Ningaloo I wasn't only reluctant to step in front of the cameras, secretly I didn't think we'd win. I thought the best we could hope for was to slow the process down and minimize damage to ecosystems. But we didn't just stop the resort entirely, we helped rewrite coastal planning regulations statewide, and eventually saw Ningaloo added to the World Heritage list.

Being a part of that campaign was an experience that brought home to me just how much attitudes had shifted. Western Australia is a politically conservative state, and yet the decision in 2003 by Premier Geoff Gallop to recognize the reef's special status was overwhelmingly popular. About a hundred thousand people got involved somehow in the defence of Ningaloo and they took the new environmental ethic seriously. Some folks might have begun to take 'greenies' a little too seriously. In October 2002 the

West Australian proclaimed that those thousands of citizens who'd declared their support for Ningaloo were part of a 'presumptuous . . . self-proclaimed environmental elite'. In the years since, right-wing columnists have regularly warned against the emergence of a dangerous new 'ruling class' from a movement they imagine to be as monolithic as it is pernicious. They decry green views as 'irrational'. Stockbroker Maurice Newman, whose wealth is largely derived from the so-called wisdom of the crowd, sees environmentalists and ninety-nine percent of climate scientists as fatally contaminated by 'groupthink'. Mining magnate Hugh Morgan has long believed the new ethos to be an essentially theological issue. The folks opposed to mining in Kakadu are apparently 'neo-pagan religious crazies and green antinomians'.[5] These magnates fear for the safety of the ruling class with which they identify and to which they cleave so faithfully, because now the nonsense of sandal-wearing no-hopers is framed in legislation, it's infected the language of business, it's taught to kids in school.

But environmentalism has not carried all before it. Power still largely resides with those for whom the war on nature is so deeply internalized the world wouldn't make sense without it. Even so, there are now conservative politicians, tycoons, miners, farmers and fishers who will quietly concede that underlying the financial market there is a larger economy to attend to. The physical facts of life – that is, the fragile and finite elements of the natural world – underpin all our endeavours. Few on the right are completely unchanged by this development in thinking, even if green activism has replaced organized labour as the political enemy. The true zealots amongst them, devotees of Ayn Rand like Gina Rinehart, have themselves begun to look like eccentrics. As if unconsciously adopting the outsider role once inhabited by Judith Wright, Rinehart has gone so far as to write poetry and organize demos.

In my own lifetime the environment has started to make the kinds of claims upon us that perhaps only family can. From the geographical ignorance and perfectly reasonable dismay of our settler forebears, we are coming, haltingly and haphazardly, to a new communal understanding. The early work of empirically minded naturalists and the specimens collected by thousands of amateurs and enthusiasts have been strengthened by generations of fieldwork in many scientific disciplines. Despite the claims of vexed tories guarding the battlements, this new ethos is not a cult. Nor is it underpinned by a misanthropic impulse – unless you believe that conceding intrinsic value to a shark or a bird is to betray your own species. Like every social movement environmentalism has its share of monomaniacs and hysterics, but at its heart is a reasonable, if sometimes disjointed, response to lived experience, disciplined study and hard-won data. Activists did not conjure collapsing fisheries, soil erosion, curdling wetlands and species extinctions from nothing. They did not invent Australia's environmental challenges. They just noticed. They paid attention to their surroundings. They acted on evidence that everyone else around them was carefully failing to recognize.

Thanks to those generations of lay interest, scientific inquiry and spirited public education, the anxiety and discomfort of our settler antecedents have given way to an affection and care they could not have foreseen. More and more of us take pride in our natural heritage. At last it seems we've begun to see past Dampier's infernal flies, to behold in our remarkable diversity of habitats, landforms and species the riches of a continental isolation that so long troubled us. Things once seen as impossibly homely, weird or simply perverse are now understood as precious. This irreplaceable organic estate informs our aesthetics and politics, our notions of pleasure and recreation. In short, it shapes our mentality. Not only have we started to integrate and internalize all these lessons, we're learning to appreciate the fragility of what sustains us.

But heartening as this change of thinking has been, it's come at a steep price. By the time we see what lies before us, much of it is compromised or ailing. It often seems that just as an ecosystem excites our interest and we start to notice its complexity, it's already collapsing. Some species of plants and animals have been expunged before we even understood what they were. This tragic pattern is yet to be outgrown. Twenty-first-century governments continue to make decisions based on the assumptions of the nineteenth century, which is one reason Australia has the highest rate of mammal extinction in the world, and why UNESCO is still keeping a wary eye on our stewardship of the Great Barrier Reef.

Still, the scruffy outliers of conservation are now suits with seats in parliament. The Greens are the third political stream in this country and in the past decade this has caused us to redefine old notions of right and left, radical and conservative, progressive and liberal. Some of the legislative outcomes have been messy. Public consensus over issues like climate change has collapsed, and with the election in 2013 of a prime minister who believes the science behind global warming to be 'crap', not even the sunniest idealist could suggest that the national mind is a steadily opening flower. There's no denying that progress is partial and incomplete, made plain by Australia's ongoing nostalgic lurch to the right. But the fact that a party putting environmental concerns at the forefront can gain seats and hold them for nearly two decades is an institutional marker for just how much our seeing – and therefore our thinking – has changed.

VI

Waychinicup, 1987

As we creep down the final hill the hidden inlet opens up to us gradually, blue and clear as a waking eye. We pause a moment to take in the view. The high sides of the valley are carpeted with heath and studded with granite boulders and vertical tors. Out at the narrow passage to the sea, swells boil against one another treacherously. But within the steep buttresses of the natural harbour the water is tranquil. The track is a bit rugged since last night's rain but it's nothing like the old days. When we reach the lumpy turnaround just above the water I park the van and the three of us get out to stretch our legs. The damp, bright shrubs are full of birds – fairy-wrens, wagtails, honeyeaters. Creek water murmurs in rivulets across the yellow-stained granites and spills onto a tiny pebble-strewn beach and our little boy wastes no time getting his shoes and pants wet. Before he was born his mother and I camped here often. When my wife was eight months pregnant with him she lowered herself into an achingly cold pool in the stream and felt him swirl and kick within her. I show our son the very pool but he's sceptical about my story. In a week he'll be three.

I've been coming to this cryptic haven since I was a teenager in Albany. At certain points of my life it's been a timely refuge. I wish we could stay a few days, but this is just a quick visit; we've made a big detour in order to stop by. Next week we're leaving the country. And I don't know why – perhaps to steel my nerves – but I need to see this place before we go.

In my youth this was a secret place for south coast locals and hard to get to. It was unmarked – you had to look for the sandy track running off at an angle from a gravel road through coastal hills fuzzed with heath. Back then an old hermit lived out here in a jauntily painted tin shack perched on a granite shelf above the water. His name was Frank Cooper. With fresh water and a plentiful supply of fish, he was pretty self-sufficient. He had a clinker-built dory, nets and a fish-smoker. Now and then a mate of his would bring out a few supplies – kerosene for his lamps, and a bit of flour, sugar and tea to keep him going. His little heeler, Blackie, slept in a tin kennel with a chaff bag nailed across the door like a curtain to keep out the rain.

Frank was basically a squatter in search of peace and quiet. In later years, when the area was declared a national park, he was allowed to stay on as its honorary ranger. He patched up the track with his wheelbarrow of marl and picked up the mess whenever kids from Albany drove out to run amok. I was a schoolboy when I first met him, one of a posse of country youths in search of a campsite free of adult surveillance. He was an old man, certainly no match for a ute-load of teenagers, but his quiet presence had a steadying effect. When I went down the track to admire his set-up he greeted me diffidently. His eyes never really met mine but he gave off an air of calm authority that intrigued me. And for years afterwards, well into adulthood, I sought him out whenever I was in the area to fish and explore the caves and thickets on the high ridges, but I couldn't say I ever got to know him. He was a shy, enigmatic fellow and he rarely said much except to comment about the tides, the weather, the state of the track and where the herring were schooling. I used to camp in a clearing only fifty metres from his place. On especially rainy days I'd lie in my tent reading Melville and Dickens with half an eye on the path, hoping he'd come by. Doubtless I was a puppy-like nuisance intruding on the space of a bloke who treasured his privacy. Local people said he'd retreated here with shell shock after his war service, but I was never sure which war he'd served in. His face was largely unlined, his age hard to determine. Most of the time he was guarded, anxious even. For such a self-reliant man he seemed strangely fragile. But once in the early 1980s I saw another side of him, relaxed and ebullient. It was a stormy winter's afternoon and a couple of his old cronies had driven out for a visit. As I passed Frank's hut that day his door stood open and his stove was aglow and so was his face. He looked like a different man. He'd a long life I knew nothing about but for a youth like me his opacity was irresistible. He never invited me into his cosy shack. I never asked him a personal question. He always affected to recognize me, but I'm sure he never knew my name.

After he grew too frail to stay on at Waychinicup, his hut was left for a while for the use of hikers and birders. But today it's gone and it's a shock to register the absence. Only the mosaic paths with their broken rims of white-wash remain. Everything else has been carted off by the rangers or the weather. As we mooch around, my wife reminisces about the large metal sunflower that stood so long in Frank's yard. Its petals were fashioned from flattened bits of tin, brightly painted, and these turned on the central axle every time a bird alighted to take the feed he'd left out. Once upon a time this place was just another part of my weird southern backstory, something my wife'd had to indulge, but now it's precious for her, too, and she was fond of Frank.

I'd always envied him – this home, his solitude. For a young man as brimful of romantic notions as I was, it was deeply affecting to behold someone so thoroughly imprinted by a place as to almost embody it. But now it's sloughing him off. In a few years there'll be no trace of him at all in this ancient landscape. Even the ringbolt he moored his dory to will have rusted away. But today the remaining signs of him are melancholy. And now that I have a wife and child his life has begun to look narrow and lonely. There must have been people he left behind, fears and sources of grief I can only guess at. Maybe Frank's exile was a form of self-medication – I'll never know.

Returning to the car we see the stack of pine logs the rangers are about to erect for barriers and signage. The ubiquitous pine log, tinged green with copper chrome arsenate, emblem of franchised domestication, even here. The heart sinks. Perhaps they're necessary. After all, people come in pretty frequently now. And yet, despite the exposure the power of the spot endures. Buried here beneath the rugged lonely hills, the tors and impenetrable thickets, this is still an enigmatic place, unsettling and unknowable. It'll always be precious to me, but it's odd, standing here, beginning to see the place in retrospect already. I'm right on site, feet on the ground and fully present, but it all feels as if it's begun to slip from my grasp. A twinge of foreboding passes through me. Will it be like this a few years hence, when we eventually fly home, the whole country suddenly faint and strange? Like any islander I feel compelled to leave, overcome with curiosity about the great world beyond. And yet as anxious as a mutineer, afraid I'm burning all boats in going.

We get back into the car, bump on up the track to the road that's been widened and sealed. We head for the highway. The coastal farms are encircled by yellow bulldozers.

The old paddocks are beginning to be ripped up for tree farms geared to tax-avoidance schemes. Mount Manypeaks shines in a distant shower of rain. The sky closes in.

We reach the highway and head for Perth. Our little boy is asleep already. All the rest of the day I catch myself peering greedily at everything, cataloguing, hoarding country, provisioning myself for the pending voyage.

The power of place

It was comically presumptuous of me, but while I was still in high school I'd begun to think of myself as a writer. At seventeen I'd never met an author. My acquaintance with the world of letters was even narrower than my experience of life, and I wish I could say I went to university to quench a raging intellectual thirst, but in truth I enrolled for the sole purpose of writing stories. In fact I approached higher education in a spirit hardly different to that of my mates who signed up at tech to learn the plumbing game, or to train as sparkies. In my mind time was too precious to spend it waffling on about Literature. I intended to *make* the stuff – with my bare hands if necessary.

So my years at university were just an excuse to hole up in a shed in my parents' backyard and write. Because the way I looked at it you learnt to write on the job, by writing. Which wasn't the most nuanced way to approach the craft of fiction, but not far wide of the mark, as things turned out. What I didn't know is that you also learn to write by watching and listening and remembering and wondering. And perhaps most importantly, by reading. As a result of four years' intensive reading I got a sort of education despite myself.

My alma mater was an institute of technology, and all the utilitarian ugliness of the label was manifested in the campus itself. The aesthetic poverty of its buildings was bewildering and oppressive. With its nasty corrugated concrete facades and industrial-park sprawl, it had the air of a wholesale storage facility. I guess it's one way of imagining a centre of learning – a bunker in which a billion units of information – bulk knowledge – are racked, stacked and filed. The interiors were worse: niggardly corridors, mean fittings, bolted aluminium windows, every seminar room reeking of cigarette smoke and nylon carpet. These chambers and halls were spaces that didn't tempt a student to linger. I certainly never dallied a moment longer than was strictly necessary. Later in life I wondered what it must have cost people to work there year upon year. Imagine twenty years trying to teach Gerard Manley Hopkins in a Bunnings Warehouse. There are hospitals, air terminals and justice complexes more congenial.

Those years I was a student I was rarely comfortable on campus and I couldn't quite commit to the institution. I was shy and a little wary, always keeping my distance, and in some ways I regret this now. It was such an exciting period – my world and my mind seemed to be glowing and expanding as never before and rarely since – and it saddens me to have so few friends from that time and such scant affection for the university itself. It might seem particularly ungracious to say this of a place with a lecture theatre named after me, but it's the truth. As the first child of my family to finish school and go on to tertiary education, and to do so in the immediate aftermath of the Whitlam enlightenment, this opportunity was precious. I always understood it was a gift, mindful that I was riding on the shoulders of two or three generations of family members taken out of school before puberty. But I never got over my physical aversion to WAIT.

In retrospect I see I was a victim of my own expectations. I'd grown up with leafier campuses in mind, like the long-established University of Western Australia whose riverside grounds at Crawley I'd walked through after picnics and prawning expeditions and in whose theatres I'd seen plays during high school. In fact I'd had an offer to study at UWA fresh out of school but in the 1970s the high-status uni made little provision for creative writing. It boasted a respectable arts course and many excellent lecturers in literature, but at the time I could only see that pathway leading to a life in the classroom and I had no interest in being a teacher, or a critic. I thought I'd leave the commentary to others. I wanted to be a player, a practitioner, and the newly established WAIT, later Curtin University, offered the country's first degree in creative writing. I was a son of the working class and I took a workmanlike mindset into seminars and workshops. I genuinely saw myself enter-ing a trade and this view was perceived as mildly eccentric by many of my teachers, and a few of my classmates. But that didn't mean I wanted to work in a factory, and that's certainly what WAIT looked and felt like.

Still, for all my reservations about the place, I prospered at university. Feeling forever out of sympathy and out of place I often worked independently, even secretively. I learnt to show certain work and withhold the rest, to participate in class but quarantine myself to some degree. I guess I didn't want to be co-opted. Perhaps, too, I didn't want to be exposed as a fake. But it meant I found my own style and subject matter in my own time, on my own terms. And I was to discover that isolation can be a boon, as much as a handicap. This is something an islander – the kind who resolves to stay and make peace with life at the margin – has to learn over time. I had several sympathetic and skillful teachers, a couple of whom were writers with an artisanal pride I instinctively understood. The most influential of these was the New Zealand writer Michael Henderson (1942–98) whose spare prose style and aesthetic passion inspired me, and under whose protection I wrote my first good stories and my first novel.

Generous study breaks between semesters gave me the chance to head south and recharge in a physical environment I loved. I dived, fished and surfed, slept in my van and read the next term's set texts under dripping canvas in a fug of wood smoke – Faulkner, Twain, Hardy, Conrad.

And in one six-week binge I tore through every Patrick White book in print, mostly on an iron bed-frame slung up in the boughs of a moort. What I responded to in these writers was the way they embraced the particulars of their place and the music of their own vernacular. I wanted to do something like that on the southern coast, which felt as if it harboured secrets and stories in every hidden cove and estuary. For all their melancholy shabbiness there was an antic spirit around some abandoned shacks and salmon lookouts. Whimsical furnishings, dunnies with sea views, hand-fashioned letterboxes where no postie had ever been. Sometimes there was nothing left but a midden of long-necks and cans, a sauce bottle, a teapot. I stumbled on the rusted trypots and remnant hearths of whalers. In deep gullies and matted clearings where the shells of a thousand feasts crunched and clattered underfoot, I sensed a profusion of resonances I didn't understand. It was like stepping into a room vacated only moments before. Everywhere unresolved events and unfinished conversations seemed to waft like the spider webs I could feel but rarely see. There were sorrows I didn't yet connect with – the absences articulated by so many Noongar names for places, creatures and plants – for the moment I was caught up with trying to find a vocabulary and a diction to match the strangeness of the places I loved and the taciturn people who inhabited them.

I was interested in spiritual retreat and contemplation in nature, and susceptible to romanticized notions of solitude, so I was curious about hermits like Frank Cooper and fascinated by the enclaves of squatters that still clung on in those days beside remote creeks and inlets. These blokes were odd-bods (for some reason they were always men). Holding out in flat-tyred caravans or tin humpies, they were not seekers or idealists so much as refugees from consequence and responsibility. Where the sand tracks petered out there were cabals of alkies, petty crims and cheapskates. Many were on the lam from the law, the tax department, their wives and their children.

But it was the real recluses who stirred my imagination, the scowling misfits in barely accessible hollows, those who retreated to the shadows until you gave up and moved on. Enchanted by Blake and Wordsworth and steeped in the eremitic characters of religious history like Simeon Stylites and Julian of Norwich, I found their stubborn isolation irresistible. Now and then one might show himself, trade a few litres of tank water for a rare carton of milk, or let slip a secret campsite for the price of a few shucked abalone or a bit of rump steak. Some consented to a few minutes

of stilted conversation. They must have wondered what
my game was, why I wouldn't just piss off and leave them
be. They looked as if they'd sprung from the lonely places
I found them in. The bowers of peppermint and tea-tree
through which they stalked and hid seemed to have shaped
their language and their personalities. Their roo-dog lean-
ness, their cragginess and their brooding silences captivated
me. I noticed the residual hints of the nineteenth century
in their vocabulary, the austerity of their expressions. These
men weren't quite modern. Some of them had a peculiar
shifting gaze, a tendency to look over my shoulder into the
damp, dark thickets pressing in from the ridges above. They
had secrets, stories they could or would not share with a
gormless kid. To me they were haunted figures in a brooding landscape, their pasts as impenetrable, as eerily palpable
as those louring thickets that hid them.

To the apprentice novelist, men like these were irresistible
characters. They gave off such a storied air. Their evasive-
ness invited invention, elaboration. I was young enough
to be startled by the living force of the past upon them.
The few I got to know were damaged men who seemed to
have reached an accommodation with themselves and their
surroundings. Some knew the poetry of Browning and
Longfellow. They spoke about French mapmakers, English

navigators and American whalers as if their ships had only minutes before cleared the headland. They alluded to ancient Aboriginal middens, springs and footpads. Their knowledge of local species was supreme. At times all these strands interwove and snagged, as if memory and lore became too dense; their train of thought broke up and skated away; they ranted or glowered or simply got up and went indoors, and in later years, reading John Clare, I associated them less with the milk-eyed seers and eccentrics of romantic poetry and thought instead of that poet's great torment in trying to hold the beloved world together in his fractured mind. For that was the thing – many of those poor old buggers were mad as meat axes, shattered by war or undone by events I was too young to comprehend. Under the brothy spell of the sublime, I invested them with a bogus nobility. To a suburban kid they seemed so special, enduring, wild and stiff-necked, in amongst the ancient rocks and gnarled trees, and while it was true enough they carried their secret places in their bodies and in their language, many simply wore their ordinary, dreary undigested pasts like rain-sodden greatcoats and lived like cripples.

Teachers of creative writing used to urge their students to write about what they know – perhaps they still do. But when you're eighteen or nineteen and keenly aware of how thin your experience really is, it's hard to put a directive like that into action. The truth is, a family and a home-town will afford you material to last a lifetime, but when you're a youth neither seems important enough to address. It's as if only distant places and other families are worth writing about. Even young New Yorkers and Londoners must feel this. For somebody writing from the wrong side of the wrong continent in the wrong hemisphere – which is more or less what it felt like when I was first writing and publishing – the feeling is acute. When you're starting out, it takes nerve to write about home and to do it in a language that's unapologetically local. Some voice in your head is telling you to moderate the demotic and the specific, to accommodate the 'cosmopolitan reader'. You waste a lot of time second-guessing this abstract stranger from somewhere far more important, and sadly, in time, you'll get to meet him or her and realize they weren't entirely imaginary. For writers at the margin there will always be an imperial pressure to relinquish particularity and conform to something more familiar, and what is most familiar to the world of publishing is an urban and largely denatured life. Whether they acknowledge it or not, many editors like to see their own lives reflected. Readers in New York and London often prefer a friction-free reading experience, so when you stubbornly write about regional lives in local vernacular you test the cosmopolitan reader's patience. These were lessons I had to learn at home before I began to be published abroad.

In the late seventies and early eighties, when I first sent stories to magazines in Melbourne and Sydney, I encountered a cultural headwind I naively assumed had puffed itself out a decade before, but despite the confidence evident in the new wave of Australian cinema, the bubbling ferment in local publishing and a fresh swagger in the arts in general, the old colonial mindset lingered on in the form of an unspoken aversion to regional settings and colloquial expression. If you were a writer or painter and you showed more than a passing interest in *place*, you risked being labelled second-rate, provincial or reactionary. Having understandably had their fill of bushrangers, hardy pioneers and Hans Heysen gumtrees, the guardians of culture were leery of anything countrified. There was a palpable anxiety about presenting a clean face abroad. Idiomatic language and settings a little alien to the inner-city milieu of publishing and cultural power bore a shaming whiff of redneck armpit. Whether you're from far north Queensland, the Territory or Western Australia, there are times when you feel as if you're living on an island within an island.

Tasmanian writers and artists live it quite literally, on an island beside an island and half the time their bit of Australia is absent from the map. And with every cultural and geographical current against you, it's hard to resist the impulse to obey the tidal logic and set sail for somewhere downwind.

As Flannery O'Connor and Alice Munro have shown, it's one thing to teach yourself to write and another to train your editors to read you. Both these regional writers – each stubbornly invested in particularity – educated their publishers and their readers with sheer persistence, by holding their nerve. Every Australian reader is forced to accommodate the strangeness of overseas – usually American or British – fictional settings. To keep up you need to adapt to new and weird idioms and soon these become normative. This provincial form of cosmopolitanism isn't optional. Similarly, a reader from some no-account place like Perth is expected to adjust their senses eastward with no reciprocity. At nineteen and twenty it was a nasty surprise to realize just how resistant a Sydney or Melbourne editor could be to the appearance on the page of Australian places and species with which they were unfamiliar. It may be hard to believe at this distance, but in my early days it wasn't just the foreign publishers suggesting I append a

glossary to the end of a novel. As I recall, the pesky dugite
(*Pseudonaja affinis*) caused the most editorial grief at home
and abroad, and I was tempted to follow St Patrick's lead
and ban elapid snakes entirely. But I kept coming back to
Flannery O'Connor. Not only was she misunderstood in
New York, she was a problem for folks at home in Georgia,
too. I loved her craft and the singularity of her world. But I
also admired O'Connor's cussedness, her refusal to come to
heel. She was an important influence.

I don't know if, in the end, I held my nerve as a writer
or just painted myself into a corner, but I persisted with
place as a starting point for all my stories. For me a story
proceeded from the logic of an ecosystem. When I began a
piece I never knew where I was headed, but I followed the
contours of the country my characters were in and found
my way to the nub of things, and over time I grew more
passionate and emboldened about using the vernacular
language of the people I knew best. In a way I wanted to
draw a reader into a fictional setting that was unmistakably distinct, just as I was swept into the foreign worlds of
Hardy's Wessex and Ronald Hugh Morrieson's Taranaki.
I began to write about Albany and the people and places
along the south coast. This was as much a matter of making
do with what I knew as it was an ongoing act of homage

to somewhere I loved. But in retrospect I see I was trying
to find a language for the presence of the past. I was coming instinctively to an understanding of the way geography
shapes us, but also tacitly giving credit to the weight of
time. When they move in and across a landscape humans
are wading through a shared past, surrounded at every
turn by events and processes that will never be over. And
I don't just mean human events, but matters of geology
and biology, too. The past is inescapable. Every extruded
stone we brush by, every flattened vowel and awkwardly
idiomatic expression we use as we stumble past it betrays
the weight of time. For someone brought up with a mod-
ernist outlook, it's hard to swallow the idea that we belong
to nature, tougher still to be owned by time.

For all Australia's blustering cultural successes in the
1980s, the old colonial anxiety about looking like yokels
in front of the wider world had not completely evaporated. When *Cloudstreet* appeared in 1991 that was still
something to contend with. By this stage I'd been writing
professionally for a decade and was for much of that time
having novels published in New York and London as well
as Sydney and Melbourne. Admittedly, with *Cloudstreet* I
was pushing vernacular as far as I could take it, to the
degree that a goodly portion of the demotic expressions

in it are entirely made up. Which was a lot of fun. But when the book was being reviewed in Australia some of the fretful critical reactions were priceless. The metropolitan contempt for regional people and their language was undisguised. After hearing an early reading in Canberra one commentator dismissed it as a throwback to *Dad and Dave*. Another lamented that I'd wasted so much time and talent on bumpkins like the Lambs and the Pickleses. Despite – or likely because of – the unexpected popularity of the novel, what troubled many critics was a potential loss of face in front of our 'betters'. Regardless of how archly some reservations were expressed, you could read two centuries of convict shame and colonial anxiety in them, as if the past were still leaning hard upon even these bright folks of the intelligentsia. I lost count of the times interviewers asked 'what they were supposed to make of it in New York'. It's painful enough to hear a question like that from your auntie on the farm, but to get it from some svelte sophisticate in seven shades of black was tragic.

Colonial stigma doesn't evaporate overnight, especially while we keep finding new ways to reproduce it, and perhaps it's deeper in our communal psyche than I care to think. Notwithstanding the forward-looking stance we like to maintain in public discourse, the past clearly bothers us, even if we're not conscious of it. Despite my conviction that non-indigenous Australians are more at home on this continent, and that progress has been made politically to address some shocking aspects of invasion and settlement, there is still a lingering unease about what lies behind, and this uneasiness is not only associated with social matters – it's also about things.

At our end of history we've come to believe we have power over nature. We like to think matter, creatures, weather and organic processes have no power over us. But if you walk deep into a wild Australian landscape, the glossy armour of your self-possession may begin to show a few cracks. Sometimes this is just a matter of scale. In several senses the sheer bulk of this country, the largeness of space, makes it unknowable. 'One seems to ride forever and come to nothing,' wrote Anthony Trollope in the nineteenth century, 'and to relinquish at last the very idea of an object.'[6] Although I celebrate the fact that our country is yet to be mastered, some creaturely part of me quails at the thought.

Much has been made of the land's so-called melancholy. Since colonial times it's been a common observation, as if there were an irresistible link between a lightly peopled continent and sadness, as if the Great South Land didn't just miss out on the Enlightenment, it wanted for company as well. But talk of a looming spirit of desolation persisted well into the twentieth century. By that time it was just as likely to be a response to the darker legacies of settlement as an expression of geographical isolation. In his wonderful history *Hunters and Collectors*, Tom Griffiths writes about the horror and shapeless depression experienced by inheritors of dispossessed lands, and he quotes ornithologist Alec Chisholm who, despite long experience in the bush, occasionally felt uneasy, 'chiefly when dusk enveloped the ridges and gullies on dull days in winter. The ironbarks now had shed their friendliness. They were, perhaps, revengeful phantoms of the black men who had once frequented these forests. Especially was I uneasy when passing a spot on a ridge-top in which white pipeclay contrasted with the sombre colour of the trees.'[7] Liminal apprehensions such as these can be hard to dismiss. Their origins are likely more than merely optical. Consider the colloquial terms for two plants – 'man fern' for *Dicksonia antarctica* and 'blackboy' for *Xanthorrhoea preissii*. Both are compact and upright and commonly grow in groups. In a lightly populated – indeed, as it frequently would have been, a depopulated – landscape, the human eye can't help but see likenesses and the mind draws on a well of communal memory. Sometimes, it seems, like the blind man of the Gospels, cured of his affliction but not yet used to his healed eyes, we still see 'men as trees walking'. Often enough the melancholy felt by settlers and their descendants was entirely their own. But for far too long such sadness was also powered by radiant absences, by silence, by guilt and denial, and until quite recently by Commonwealth law.

Still, it seems fair to admit that the land itself could be implacable. It did not readily admit interlopers.

When I look at sepia images of my forebears they appear apprehensive. Some arrived in chains, others were settlers. On their camel-drawn sulkies or leaning against tree stumps and rough huts, they narrow their eyes defensively at the camera. For some the strangeness of this country was too much. At least one lost his mind and retreated to a cupboard to hang himself. Many others seem to have been brave, hardy people. They don't have the ebullient faces of settlers in the American west, for dogged as they were they lacked the optimism and sense of manifest destiny of those on the American frontier. This isn't only about the disgust and disenchantment of the newcomer: my ancestors looked fearful. And they were probably right to be. All the landscapes they settled in or were consigned to by the Crown were places of great and abiding power, and that potency has not diminished.

For one thing, the evidence of death is everywhere in this country: shells, bleached bones, the emu woven through five strands of fence-wire. And it's an ongoing process: trees turning to dust before your eyes as termites grind them into soil, skittled bullocks pumping themselves into bloated travesties at the roadside. A constantly poised potential: the telltale chicken-wire bubbles of a croc in a billabong, the wispy translucence of the box jellyfish glistening in the throw-net.

Some places simply feel too tough for humans. Capstone moonscapes in which a feral goat might struggle to keep its feet. Gibber plains where the light is insufferable. Tea-tree thickets that sap your will to live. There are places that feel uncongenial for reasons you know are irrational. Some-times it's more about being alone in them that's suddenly giving you the creeps. Camped at the samphire edge of a birrida – a sort of gypsum claypan – near Shark Bay many years ago, I was overcome by a fear of inundation. The sea was kilometres off in the distance and hadn't been this way in centuries but when I lay on my swag the land felt too low to be trusted. It's one thing to lie on a riverbank under a sheet at night listening to saltwater crocodiles ambushing barramundi a few metres below you, but to toss and turn at the prospect of an ancient sea returning when there's nothing out there but crickets is ridiculous.

All the same, plenty of natural threats are real enough. To stand in a tingle forest in even a moderate breeze is to experience a force no research can prepare you for. With their giant, fire-hollowed buttresses and restless crowns, these trees creak with enough pent-up energy to make your flesh crawl. How my ancestors must have hated trees: the wandoo that burps sparks at the blow of an axe, the relentless thickets of peppermint and stubborn jam, the groaning armies of karri massed upon ridges as far as the eye can see. Whether you're at war with them or you come in peace, trees can be genuinely malevolent presences. In a high wind they're dangerous and at dusk they're untrustworthy. It's not just when they're spitting embers that they seem carnivorous. The fires of yesteryear have left them riven with gaping, grinding mouths that can snap shut and bring down the night sky in a moment.

The animated landscape of Aboriginal Australians is not fanciful. Landforms, plants and bodies of water possess the sort of power that's palpable to even an heir of industrialized scientism like me. In this country, outside the cities especially, it takes a certain determination to ignore the

THE POWER OF PLACE

ardour and livid energy at work in nature. The studious disenchantment of a modern education is no protection against it. Some of it is just lingering force, a constant trail of evidence. Like the massive boab tree rent in half by lightning, or the barnacle-encrusted boulders you discover on the clifftop high above the sea after a cyclone. But a lot of Australia's might is experienced in real time. In the desert you feel the country forsake its mild mood soon after dawn, and as it works itself up into its noonday rage the birds fall nearly silent, the reptiles retreat and the spinifex seethes and sweats its cloying musk. Everything around you is pushed to its absolute limits, tested to within an inch of its life.

At times you perceive this force as something passive, at others as a kind of intransigence, but along with the grinding authority of inertia and attrition, places exert active, unpredictable power, a lively and sometimes fickle agency my Kentish and Irish antecedents – like the continent itself, largely untouched by the apparent Good News of the Enlightenment – would probably have affirmed without hesitation. On every continent, places both wild and built still brim with power. Things have their own secret histories and inner lives. Europeans know this – they sense it most keenly in buildings. You can't help but feel an afterglow of the past in the stone flags of a castle keep from the Dark Ages or the ruins of a Roman house beneath the streets of Paris, but it's palpable in nature, too. When you hike up through a rocky island pass in Greece as olive prunings are being burnt you can literally smell spent time – you taste it. Closer to home I've witnessed the queer violence an Indonesian sea cave can assert as it vomits bats at dusk. The awe of traditional people in places like these should not be surprising.

For all our delusions of technological mastery and our beetle-browed fixation on the future, citizens of the developed world can still be cowed by the presence of the past. Sometimes your senses are distorted by 'mere' geology. In a desert gorge, say, where hot rocks blow frigid air from karst vents and every baking, parched stone bears the counterintuitive scars of water. Walking through old mine diggings where land has been laid waste forever, I feel a queasiness, a sense of reproach so direct it seems to come from the place itself. And I don't believe my sorrow and agitation are only projection, for these feelings are not so different to the creeping shame and awe you're subject to at the scene of any violent crime. You feel the dead, the afterglow of experience.

But experience is not exclusive to humans. Country

lives too, it strives and yearns and changes. And maybe it remembers, for the past is never over. Not even for stones and water. Particularly not for these. I've been to places in the Pilbara and the Kimberley where hidden soaks and sudden breakaways give off a watchfulness, a discomforting presence not easily accounted for. You ask yourself: Did something terrible happen here? Or is this resonance just a signal of the life force in the country? In spots like these it can be a relief to find evidence of ancient culture because it makes some sense of the uncanny sensation. The petroglyph, the rubbing stone or ochre painting lets you off the hook. You can reassure yourself that someone else has felt this before you. So perhaps you're not imagining it. But then you wonder: Am I feeling the people of this place or the power they've always found in it? I suspect at times even a non-indigenous visitor might catch an echo of both. Looking on wryly, an Aboriginal Australian may not even credit the distinction. Either way it's hard to imagine, even where custom and law have been fatally interrupted and there are no physical remnants of arts or industry, that a human history of sixty thousand years will never make its presence felt in country that appears to be otherwise bereft of people.

There are, of course, many places in Australia where

this primal energy has been known since time imme-morial and where it continues to be refreshed by ritual visits and ceremonial relationship. My acquaintance with these kinds of places is largely restricted to the far north Kimberley, home to the world's oldest extant tradition of icon painting. In rock shelters throughout coastal archi-pelagos, behind mainland beaches and out into a rugged hinterland the size of California, the conjoined pasts of people and country endure and continue in sites of rare power. Here the Ngarinyin, Wunambal and Worora peo-ples have been painting and maintaining their mouthless Wandjina figures since the beginning of human history. Daubed in ochre, these images of fierce, life-giving, watch-ful energy stare out from ledges and adorn cave ceilings. Their companions, the smaller Gwion Gwion figures that dance along lintels and walls close by, are further evidence of how long and how intimately this remotest country has been known and revered. When a traditional lawman approaches a Wandjina site he is often a mixture of cau-tion and suppressed excitement. He announces himself and his companions as if to a relative of great standing. Like all icons, the Wandjina craves company. It is revived and enlarged by attention. The elder's visit replenishes its power. As of this writing there are still pre-contact lawmen in the

region carrying on an ancient and sacred tradition of recip-
rocation that secures a place and its people. An outsider is
tempted to look upon these paintings as mere artworks, but
they're much more than that. Similarly the non-indigenous
visitor is likely to be overcome by the antiquity of these
sites, when for those who maintain and are maintained by
them they are living places where past, present and future
are indistinguishable.

On a continent where native mammal extinctions are
rivalled only by extinctions of indigenous languages and
cultures, the fragile persistence of the people of the Wandjina is something to treasure and to celebrate. Indeed,
Kimberley rock art has garnered passionate and influential
non-indigenous enthusiasts. But although many are keen to
preserve what they view as artifacts of antiquity, they're far
less passionate about the sacred power and ongoing cultural
role these sites retain for living people, fellow citizens whose
existence only makes sense because of them and whose
health and wellbeing depend upon contact with and attention to them. Too few rock art enthusiasts and specialists in
the academy value the custodians of these sites beyond their
initial use as guides and 'informants'. The cultural expertise
of traditional owners continues to be scandalously under-
valued.[8] Wealthy lessees of cattle stations where much of

this art is situated, many of whom were introduced to it through the Bush University of the Ngarinyin, and who later formed a foundation for its protection, have in recent years been accused of restricting access to the rock art on their leases to an exclusive social set. That is to say, they make a trophy of another people's living culture. In the wake of Native Title deliberations, there are regular reports of traditional owners being barred entry to these sites.[9] The implication is clear enough: the paintings are more precious than the people who make them. Perhaps another instance where the colonial past has not been shaken off.

Since those early years of my apprenticeship, the effect of the power of place on the behaviour and aspirations of the people around me has been my underlying and ongoing concern. Others had been there before me, of course. In *Voss*, Patrick White's expeditionary hero ventures out into the hinterland to conquer distance. He aims to master country and fill its apparent emptiness by his sheer presence, with his ego and his sense of European destiny. In the end he's swallowed operatically by desert, a victim of his own ignorance. *Voss* was a turning point for me, a sign of what might be possible in writing poetically about figures in landscape. But closer to home, Randolph Stow was the greater influence. I came upon *The Merry-Go-Round in the Sea* as a schoolboy and loved it, but *Tourmaline* and *To the Islands* were books that excited me the way few novels have, before or since. Stow was a native of Geraldton, my mother's hometown. When I was eighteen it was barely conceivable that a genius such as this might spring from a rough old midwest town like the one I knew and where my cousins lived. Even though they sprang from an earlier era – like my parents, Stow was born in the 1930s – his novels were the first in which I recognized my own land and people without having to translate and accommodate as I read. White and Stow were both sons of the squattocracy but Stow reached an intimacy with the natural world that the more celebrated laureate never could.

Heriot, the raging apostate pilgrim of *To the Islands,* has long been a teacher, protector and controller at his far-flung mission. His aims are in keeping with those of the racist mid-century government and he fears change – fresh policy directions and a new sense of agency amongst the tribal people for whom he is accountable. And Heriot, of course, goes to pieces. On the face of it, his trajectory is not unlike Voss's. An angry failure, perhaps even a murderer, he journeys out into the remotest bush in what looks like an act of self-destruction. But the teacher finds himself brutally taught, strangely protected and militantly controlled by the country he blunders through. At the end he relinquishes the idea of an object. He surrenders to immensity and merges with the landscape, turning a European *failure to arrive* into a tragic antipodean acceptance, even an apotheosis. To me it's a visionary work. Stow is still the marker for me, the distant knoll by which I take my bearings. Whether writing of the ghost-ridden midwest of his youth, the febrile Trobriand Islands of his years as a patrol officer or the enchanted landscape of his long, self-imposed exile in Suffolk, he was sensitive to landscape in a way few other prose writers, of any country, have been. For years I mourned his lingering late-life silence. But now I wonder if such a reticence wasn't inevitable. While he seemed to feel the country of his birth as if he wore it, the nation-state he left behind pushed on as if the frontier ethos were all the inspiration a people could desire. More and more, it must have seemed that he was speaking a different language.

I was so young when I first began publishing fiction that for a long while I felt I had no peers. All I mean by that is I'd gotten a head start on my own generation and for a decade or so, before writers my age like Gillian Mears and Richard Flanagan and others came along, I felt a little isolated. So, with characteristic cheek, I privately claimed Stow as a peer. After all, he'd begun writing and publishing when startlingly young, and he was, at least in his youth, a local. I never met the man. But he was good company. I will always be in his shadow.

VII

Northam, 1995

Spread below us, the land is flat and golden, all its undulations etched into shadow. Wheat stubble is sectioned into orderly rectangles. Sheep pads spider away from dams and troughs. From above, the windmills are barely visible. Rare clumps of trees stand in vivid contrast to the bleached summer pastures. When sheep move, as hot milk spilt across a tawny cloth, dust rises like steam in their wake.

The little plane vibrates. Despite myself, I stare distractedly at the pilot's long, painted nails and the way her pewter shoes shuffle the pedals. Who was I expecting to fly this thing, Tony Bonner from *Skippy*? I should be ashamed of myself. Though I'm slightly bilious, if that counts as suitable mortification.

We shudder through an updraught and Richard Woldendorp, the laureate of Australian aerial photography, reaches forward and taps the pilot on the shoulder. Without even a nod she tips the plane to starboard and Richard opens his window. Hot wind rips through his thin scurf of hair. He thumbs his specs back and hefts his big lens through the gap. As we turn circles across the dusty paddocks, he hangs half out of the window, this portly man in his late sixties, and clacks away until he's satisfied. Few can have put in as many flying hours in the cause of art.

Born in Utrecht in 1927, Woldendorp arrived in Australia in 1950 and has been compulsively shooting landscape from the air for half a century. He says that it's from here, in the sky, that he most experiences 'a sense of wonderment of a world so complex, varied and beautiful'. After fifty years you'd expect him to be hard to please, but even this depleted pastoral landscape brings out an impish excitement in him. He's fascinated by the way the landforms below seem to mimic the patterns and shapes of so many creatures and objects you encounter at ground level. At first glance his photographs can look like abstract-expressionist paintings. I've seen the double-takes they produce in corporate lobbies, airport lounges and museums across the country.

We drop and lurch and yaw. He aims and bangs away again and my gut begins to stir. It's not comfortable watching the man work, but it's an honour all the same.

When we even out again I feel the first cold sweats, but Richard reloads, waits. We bank out over a dam and as the sun catches its surface it flashes silver, hard and bright as an accusation. I glance back at Richard. He gives a boyish gap-toothed grin, a thumbs-up. I wish he hadn't told me on the drive out about the forced landing on the saltpan at Lake Eyre, or wherever it was. But I return the gesture as if I'm perfectly at home.

The downward view

I was twenty-one before I flew in an aeroplane. Still at
university and halfway through a second novel, I was travelling to Sydney to collect a prize for the one I'd written a
year before. And it was startling, seeing the country from
the air for the first time. How flat the hilly jarrah forests

were from above, how relentless the bitumen highway heading east. The wheatbelt looked so organized and geometrical
and even the remnant woodlands at its edges were as rigidly
defined as carpet cuttings. But none of that imposed order
could resist the meandering loops and dints of the salt that
was beginning to encroach on agriculture. The wheatland
looked like a hard-worn shirt rimed with fractals of dried
sweat. Soon the familiar Southern Ocean fell into view near
Esperance. A road trip of ten hours reduced to minutes. So
often a maelstrom at the surface and a killing field below it,
the sea looked as safe and baby-blue as an infant's blanket.
Out along the Bight in South Australia, surf foamed and
boiled against the Bunda Cliffs. I'd stood down there as a
kid and heard the hellish roar, but from an altitude of ten
thousand metres the spectacle was silent and tame and the
vicious whitecaps off Port Lincoln, where tuna boats toiled
in a rugged chop, looked about as menacing as dandruff.

Seeing the land from the air will probably always be
strange, but then it's a relatively new perspective for humans.
And it still seems an outrageous privilege. Altitude transforms landscape entirely. From up there, as landforms and
vegetation groups overlap and dissolve into one another, you
see the geological and hydrological connections that go to
make a place. Relieved of human and terrestrial limitations

you glimpse vast distances in a single moment. You're suddenly angelic, safe from the land and its carnal logic. How puny trees are at altitude when at ground level they humble and impress as colonies and sanctuaries, as monuments to life. From the air they can be reduced to texture, or mere territory like the abstract stuff of maps. Rendered thus, country looks so much more expendable, so open and welcoming of extraction. A forest looks so loggable and a red range so exploitable. The aerial perspective doesn't always reveal intrinsic beauty.

Indeed, for a long time the aerial perspective has been a vital tool of commodification, a means of turning land into money. The iron barons of the Pilbara love to recount the flights that supposedly sparked their fortunes. Some, as in Lang Hancock's oft-told account, have begun to sound a little too mythical to be taken literally, but unquestionably there were mesas and canyons in the Pilbara that were doomed the moment men like him buzzed over them in Cessnas. Within a generation the same process familiar to coastal Australia was under way, only at greater speed and intensity as landforms, ecosystems and sacred places were transformed into mere ore deposits. As Hancock is quoted as saying, 'Nothing should be sacred from mining, whether it's your ground, my ground, the blackfellow's or anyone else's.'[10] The man who suggested the government should 'dope up' the water supplied to Aborigines so as to render them sterile was in no doubt about what this country signified and who it rightfully belonged to. He made his fortune from dirt but he saw the land from on high, which is a polite way of saying his perspective on the living world and his fellow humans was resolutely downward.

Sometimes it pays to be sceptical of the aerial view. From a sufficient height, Uluru itself can look no more remarkable than a stale school bun. In the far northern Kimberley I have emerged from coastal country so rugged and difficult that cars are useless and traversing it on foot is gruelling, if not impossible, and yet the moment the seaplane lifts you away from the beach or the chopper plucks you off the ridge, the same terrain looks pretty, harmless, inviting. Within seconds you've gone from earthbound defeat to celestial transcendence and the higher you fly, the less human your view.

Buzzing low, as Woldendorp does, at least you're close enough for trees to remain trees. Jump-ups and gorges retain their three-dimensional reality. At such a modest altitude you feel more birdlike and less disembodied and you see accordingly. The smoke of bushfires fills the cockpit. The heat of all those stones still reaches you. The terrain is not so distant as to become wallpaper. As the biologist Charles Birch would say, things remain subjects, not objects.

From just above the treetops the skin of the land looks creaturely, like the hide of a crocodile, the pelt of a kangaroo, the feathers of corellas, the bark of boabs. It's organic; its life is still legible. Where wind and water have flayed the soil for aeons, you see the country's bones. The continent is so beaten down it looks threadbare, but obdurate too, long-suffering in its great age, hanging on despite every natural and human force laying siege to it. Where it seems defeated from the air it's often holding out at ground level. Crossing country that shows no sign of rain you come upon a cataract. In niches and hidden gullies of fire-blackened mesas and ridges there are sudden patches of rainforest seething with birds.

But there's no doubting the utility of the aerial perspective, especially on a continent as large and relatively unpeopled as ours, where down at the surface the larger ecosystems are hard to take in as anything but abstractions. A reef or river system or a savannah is both immense and immensely complex in its constituent parts, and without overflying something so enormous it's hard to conceptualize. Sometimes there's nothing like seeing things in one seraphic sweep. Flying above the vast shallows of Shark

Bay, for instance, with their dazzling, mottled meadows of seagrass, is to quickly feel an outlandish notion become manifest. So, you soon think, that's what fourteen thousand square kilometres of estuary looks like. One small section, the Wooramel Seagrass Bank, is the largest structure of its kind in the world. In a few moments you see why Shark Bay was classified as a World Heritage area.

Like Richard Woldendorp, I love to see nature echoing itself: the way longshore drift leaves a pattern of scalloping on beaches that replicates the shape and texture of the very shells that wash up on their shores. These recurrences appear in totally unrelated landscapes. The pointillism of spinifex on pindan plains is repeated in a different palette in dry sclerophyll forests; the pebble-dash maze of a gibber plain seen at roo-rousing altitude is repeated at a thousand feet over a coral reef, where each 'stone' is a lump the size of a Haulpak truck.

Many flyers make the false connection between aerial landscapes and Aboriginal paintings from the desert schools. Artists from Utopia, for instance, are not depicting aerial views at all, but they do repeat shapes, patterns and motifs that are everywhere in nature, some of which represent deep story, biological relationships and cultural information not easily available to those not born to the desert. Even so, it's tantalizing that the most earthbound artists on the continent should appear to be seeing and painting the earth from the sky.

For the rest of us, Australia is probably most familiar from the air. Living in a country so vast, this is generally how we travel across it, how we gain any sense of scale and linkage, how we understand it, and quite literally how we govern it. But it's a mistake to equate familiarity with intimacy. Commuting over plains, deserts, woodlands and ranges at ten thousand metres, we flatter ourselves when we assume we know what it is we're seeing.

VIII

Mitchell Plateau, 1993

After a week's barramundi fishing it's time to get the plane out. I'm in dire need of a shower and so are my friends. My hair and clothes have gone mouldy. My legs are stippled with insect welts and my hands smart from a hundred tiny perforations from spines and hooks. To get to the airstrip up on the plateau we need to cross the gulf by boat and make it up the washed-out track by noon. At dawn I'm staring down the gulf toward the escarpment as I finish my coffee. The strip is only five kilometres away but it'll take half a day to reach.

In the wet-season glass-off the boat ride is dreamy, almost surreal. The air is damp and warm. The hull's glide feels frictionless, and glimpsed through the patches of rainforest above the mangroves, at the confluence of the Lawley and Mitchell rivers, the ramparts of the plateau are banded with horizontal layers of rosy bauxite that miners have been trying for a generation to exploit, against the wishes of traditional owners. The bluffs and approaches are striped with ephemeral waterfalls flashing silver in the early light.

From the dinghy we stagger up the pebble beach through a merciless welter of sandfleas. The boxy old short-wheelbase Land Cruiser is there beneath its tarp. We fire it up and begin the long, arduous climb in low range. At this time of year, in the waning wet, the track is more or less a watercourse. The ascent is achingly slow and a little perilous. Against an axle-deep stream, at angles that don't bear thinking about, the vehicle crawls across slimy rocks and logs that thud and grind against the diffs. Now and then, when the wheels lose traction, it yaws off the track and drifts free until we're stranded on the scree-slope. Then we step out gingerly to lever it back across in stages with the high-lift jack. It's sweaty work and nerve-racking.

It takes a couple of hours to cover the first two kilometres. Then the track grows firmer and we actually make second gear. Eventually we reach level ground up on the plateau proper where everything is a mad profusion of growth, hot and wet, and the journey turns into a total inversion of the standard car ride. We pick up speed, trundling blindly through the head-high spear grass, between pandanus and livistona palms, still safely beyond the barrier of glass and steel, but soon the cab is too stuffy to bear and we roll down the windows and let come what may. The track is entirely obscured, the view literally ends at the bullbar, but we allow the front wheels to seek the unseen ruts and the vehicle more or less steers itself. As we mow down the wall of grass and vines, grasshoppers, moths, dragonflies and birds peel upward from it in vivid rushes. Bugs and grubs, mantises and spiders gather in our hair, sucking the perspiration on our faces, catching in the gaps in our teeth. The air is soupy. The whole plateau is choking with life and we chug against this mad plenitude like a boat in a sluggish, druggy sea. Everything around us fizzes and swirls psychedelic on the wing. The country feels too warm, too thick, too wild and rich to be real. My skin prickles and crawls. The livid world folds away in my path like the sea before Moses. And then we're through, pressing out onto the open swathe of slashed ground. The gravel strip is flat and neat, walled in by jungly green.

The plane is waiting. The pilot emerges from the shade of the wing. His epaulettes are crisply aligned, the fuse-lage gleams behind him. We climb out to greet him but I haven't quite reached his timezone yet. There are still wings inside my shirt, legs in my hair. I'm spitting green ants and ladybirds, like a traveller from another world entirely.

* In March 2015 Rio Tinto and Alcoa announced they were relinquishing their joint-venture plans to mine bauxite on the Mitchell Plateau. The West Australian government declared it would reserve five million hectares there, making it 'Australia's largest national park'. On that short and surreal journey in 1993 I could never have imagined this outcome.

The steel cocoon

For a few summers when I was a kid we used to drive from Perth to Greenough, just south of Geraldton, to stay near the mouth of the river in a beach shack that belonged to relatives. In February the trip was so hot we took to driving it at night. We never had a car with airconditioning – we travelled with the windows down. Mum made a nest of sheets and pillows on the back seat of the FC Holden and the three of us kids snuggled down and saw nothing until we arrived at dawn. Even now there are towns on that Midlands road that I don't know at all – Carnamah, Three Springs, Mingenew – because I only ever passed through them at night. In those days before the Brand Highway was built it was a long, roundabout trip that could take up to seven hours and in memory it often feels as if I smelt my way there, because I can still smell all those freshly harvested paddocks, the treacherously dry wild oats at the roadside, and the baked desert wind blowing across the domestic scents of upholstery and clean linen. Eventually, as light leaked into the sky, the telling aroma of sea salt and *Olearia axillaris* (the coastal daisy we grew up calling saltbush) heralded our arrival.

My own kids seem to cavil at the prospect of a long drive – too many weeks spent bouncing in the back of a troopy, I imagine. Even the dog needs to be coaxed aboard these days. And the grandkids are still at the age when a car journey sends them to sleep in minutes. But as a boy I looked forward with enormous excitement to a proper road trip. And without doubt, the biggest adventure of my childhood was the trek we made across the Nullarbor in the summer of 1969–70 before the road was sealed. During that Christmas holiday we crossed the continent, coast to coast. It was a season like no other, an insight into just how big and strange our country was. But the highlight for me, with all its peculiar initiatory ordeals and sensations, was the treeless plain itself. It was a 1200-kilometre leg, most of it flat and straight, and more than half of it done on a limestone track rough enough to shake the fillings from your teeth. There were wrecked cars and exploded caravans at the roadside. Vehicles blew by with shredded tyres lashed to their roof racks, and before they were swallowed in chalky white dust, fellow travellers gave us a jaunty thumbs-up as if to stiffen our resolve. Because it was hard going. But groan and growl as we did, jouncing around in the back of the Hillman Hunter station wagon, a part of us welcomed the discomfort. It made us feel like intrepid expeditioners, as if the trials of the journey were making us more ruggedly authentic, more Australian.

Of course, though we were pummelled from dawn till dusk, coughing and sneezing all the way, we spent the bulk of the trip literally sealed inside the shell of the vehicle. Acting on a tip-off at Eucla, Dad taped the doors and windows shut. Even so, the dust was unstoppable, and in a sense this was the only part of the landscape we really engaged with.

It wasn't until we pulled over at day's end that we truly felt the singularity of the place. From inside the car the scale of the landscape didn't seem so freakishly big, but outside it I felt my mind struggling to keep up with the endless openness. It was exciting, and a little frightening. Set free from the vehicle we were like hens released from a battery cage, cautiously testing the ground underfoot, uncertain of our parameters, sniffing the bluebush and tasting gravel dust on our tongues. I remember standing over the weird mesmerizing vortex of a blowhole as it siphoned the distant sea air into the desert. Some evenings as we sat, road-stunned, to eat our baked beans and Rice Cream, a great stillness settled upon us and for a while it sounded like silence. Until the cryptic sounds of the plain made it past the fading roar in our ears. Tiny birds spritzed about in the saltbush, skinks and marsupials stirred unseen in the darkening mulga. What had seemed empty and desolate was actually alive, twitching, chattering, sighing and questing high and low. It had been all day, of course. The difference was we'd stopped moving long enough to hear.

Automobiles are a boon. They have liberated us from drudgery and brought us an ease of movement once unthinkable. In a single week I can visit places my forebears might have spent two lifetimes searching out. Our journeys are largely free of the suffering and danger that were once bound up in travel. A suburb like the one I grew up in would have been untenable, perhaps even inconceivable, without the assumption that every household in it was supported by a motor vehicle. In the first half of the twentieth century automobiles augmented our settlements, now they shape them, determining where they're situated, how they're laid out. Our cities are built to accommodate the car as much as the citizen, and the outward creep of low-density suburbs is the unsustainable price we pay for our enviable new mobility. Even our homes, with their integrated garages, have been steadily modified – disfigured in many instances – to adapt to the primacy of vehicles in domestic life.

But the pity of this gift is that in the hinterlands, as in the cities, we defer too much to our machines. As with the mobile phone and the personal computer, we let cars master us. We don't just let them determine what we'll see by the speeds and routes we travel, sometimes the driving and the vehicle become ends in themselves. How often have you foregone a stop for fear of losing time or needing to make it up? I'm a shocker for this. A long trip gives me road fever; I'm forever anxious to press on, keep going. I can sit fourteen hours a day behind the wheel on an open road. There's a kind of gorging impulse, as if I'm eating the distances, kilometre by kilometre, even if I'm on a journey without a deadline or a fixed destination. The not-so-funny joke in my family is the standard reply I offer a passenger dying for a pee. 'What's your problem?' I invariably ask. 'We stopped four hours ago.'

I've seen a hell of a lot of landscape through the car window, most of it viewed at speed in bleary, lazy glimpses, like all those drowsy hours of TV with the world running past in a one-dimensional format, segmented and edited for passive, casual and non-absorbent viewing. On the couch or behind the wheel I glance outward, but I'm not sure how much I really see. Thanks to airconditioning most of us no longer smell the peculiar scents of places; we hear no birds, feel no wind. We're mostly oblivious to fluctuations in temperature. You register little more than the noise of the engine and the soundtrack you've brought with you. You travel too fast to notice many creatures. Sometimes you recognize a native mammal only the second before you reduce it to roadkill. Seeing the country by car, you may think you're in the landscape but really you're in geographical limbo. Enclosed in your steel cocoon you experience the car first, the place you're in comes a distant second.

While for the driver the car is a personal fiefdom, for

the passenger it may be another matter. That's a lesson I learnt the summer of our great road trip. I was carsick at Glenrowan, hungry and miserable all along the Great Ocean Road, and I bickered incessantly with my brother through the Riverina. Like him and my little sister I was making none of the navigational choices. We were captives, as my own kids were hostages in their way along the bush tracks of the Dampier Peninsula and the Gibb River Road. That Christmas trip of 1969–70 I saw a fair bit of Australia. But I saw even more motor car.

Happily a lot of country is vivid enough to penetrate the shell of the vehicle and stir the driver from his trance. You notice grasstrees massed like warriors in their thousands. Half an hour later you're in a plain of limestone pinnacles like a war cemetery and the conjunction sets your mind racing.

I was driving south from the Pilbara one morning, keen to catch a radio signal in the minutes before the national news bulletin, when I noticed lines of ancient dunes stacked away to the horizon, huge and uniform as storm swells marching in from a distant sea. Stones glittered at their tawny crests like the sheen of sun on water and I drove and stared, so entranced by this oceanic mirage that when the radio finally came to life it startled me to such a degree that

I swerved like a madman and nearly put myself into the mulga.

But a car can also render the outlandish mundane. The first time you encounter a saltpan the size of a city you may slow down and exclaim, but at the speed you're travelling there'll be three or four others along pretty soon; your gaze may well be outward and interested, but after that initial silver-pink shock you'll barely notice them. Even the tortured river red gums on the Greenough floodplain become domestic detail after you've driven by a hundred times. Genuflecting grotesquely before the perpetual southerly, they are almost unrecognizable as representatives of their species, *Eucalyptus camaldulensis*. There's something lurid and expressionistic about their growth patterns, the way they toil like hemiplegics, trunks bent at right angles, parallel to the earth, crowns kissing the dark soil before them. They were livid presences in my childhood, weird haunting figures amid the still-standing ruins of the floods of 1888, but these days, unless I'm travelling with a newcomer to the midwest, I can often pass by without noticing them at all. It's not just repetition making things like these indistinct, it's the inhuman speed at which we travel.

When I see long-distance cyclists grinding away at the roadside, their swags and billies strapped behind them as they pump and shine along the highway's perilous edge, I find myself embarrassed to be moving so effortlessly. I can't help but defer to the laborious authority of their progress. We're each travelling through the same land-scape, these mad bastards and I, but surely their experience is deeper, more authentic. They must absorb things I miss entirely: if I had any substance I'd be down there at the gravel-strewn shoulder, pedalling away with them. In the toxic gusts of diesel smoke and the slamming slipstream of roadtrains a hundred metres long. I envy these intrepid pedallers but my admiration is only momentary. It's fine thinking of the journey itself as the destination but there's a lot to be said for safe arrival.

Still, you're not really anywhere much at all until you climb out of the car, and even a white-line-fever fiend like me will occasionally remind himself to break a day's driving and pay attention to something memorable along the way. Headed for the far north Kimberley one winter I pulled up beside the vast tidal mudscape of King Sound, near Derby. I'd been on the road two days straight with a couple still ahead of me and I could feel my mind and body growing numb, so I stopped awhile to watch the tide go out along the delta. A spring tide is dramatic anywhere but there are few tidal events as spectacular as what you'll see at Derby when the moon is full and all that chocolate water gets moving. From the car it was quite a picture but outside the vehicle it was a reeking tumult. I'm glad I spared the hour to take it in properly. The energy of the tide was colossal. The outward flow was so strong it wasn't hard to imagine the last dampness underfoot, the very moisture of your body, being sucked out along with it. As slick brown water retreated from the mangrove ramparts it seemed to flee the land in a headlong stampede, flaying the trees that flashed olive green and then tawny and silver as they shivered and creaked, clutching at one another to survive the force of it. A million snarls of roots began to show and then canyons of mud, foetid and spidered with runnels and sucking pits. It popped and blurted, fizzing with skippers and the crone fingers of pneumatophores. Within minutes the flooded forest looked like somewhere you could venture into. But I knew better than to try. It wasn't just the crocs giving me pause, it was the thought of foundering chest-deep in mullock, being tasted and swallowed whole, stuck there, unable to move and slowly sinking from view as the stereo pumped out Steely Dan up there behind me on dry land.

I stayed put. I gave up struggling to take it in visually and just listened. The place was teeming. I heard, far off, the wingbeats of a brahminy kite. Then, closer, the sudden

ka-boosh of a barramundi monstering a mullet in a chan-
nel. And finally it was so quiet I caught something else, an
unsettling chain of whispers, and when I opened my eyes I
saw it was a leafball of green ants, suspended from a wild fig
nearby. I leant in and there it was, plain and clear, a steady
chickering noise like gossip.

IX

Cape Range, 2009

When the track becomes impassable I climb down, leave the vehicle and hike up beyond the eerie pink monuments of the termite mounds into the first ridges fanning out from the canyon mouth. Eventually there's no red soil left at all, only red and blond marl and plates of shifty shale surrounded by spinifex. Because I'm alone and a great distance from help, I walk with the kind of elaborate care that inevitably renders a person clumsy. Just navigating is challenge enough. For the moment I'm not seeing much more than my evenly laced boots but I don't want to twist an ankle on this unstable ground or step on a death adder coiled in the spinifex shadows. It's hypnotic, though, the excess concentration. I follow my feet up the slope like a dolt who's never seen his own boots before.

I'm looking for black-flanked rock-wallabies. They're a small, agile species with a racy tricoloured face. Their numbers have been decimated by foxes and in Western Australia only half a dozen robust populations still exist in the wild. They favour high, rocky country and here they have an ocean view with the coral sprawl of Ningaloo Reef at their feet. I like to come up into these red ranges to sit and watch them, but they're skittish and I'm covering a lot of open ground with the wind at my back. I travel as quietly as I can but on loose pebbles it's hard to be stealthy.

I choose a gully radiating from the main gorge and crunch slowly up its stony bed, climbing through vine snares and leggy nests of wild fig. It's a winter's day and mild for these parts but I've already sweated through my shorts and T-shirt. From here the incline only steepens. Up ahead

the red-pink bluffs rise against a cloudless sky. The landscape is parched. All the plants are semi-arid miniatures,
from the desert pea to the waist-high kurrajongs. There's
no suggestion of water anywhere and yet everything I see
has been formed by torrents. The range is remnant reef and
ancient uplift but the ragged surface is the work of cyclonic
rains. The gouges and gutters I pick my way up are older
than human time but the dams of shale that choke them
could be as recent as last year. Underfoot, in silent darkness,
mysterious stygofauna swim and bristle. The entire range is
honeycombed with freshwater caves, forming an elaborate
limestone karst system of a scale and richness that beggars
belief.

Across the shin-high scrub a black-faced cuckoo-shrike
flits past. Zebra finches animate the middle distance like
midges. I'm elevated enough for the breeze to cool the sweat
on my back. I try to resist thinking about water.

I stop a moment and scan the breakaway with binoc-
ulars. A white-bellied sea-eagle tips out over the canyon.
A few euros prop and pitch along the ridge, bobbing against
the pale spinifex like rosy stones hurling themselves uphill.
No black-flanks are visible for the moment. At this time
of day they seek whatever shade is offered by a small tree
or a boulder. I'll need to be patient. I'll climb as high as

possible to watch and wait. From here I can see the dark mouth of a cave beneath the brow of the bluff. I pack the glasses away and aim for it, following the narrow, winding pad and the telltale scat. In the end, faced with a crenellated barrier of boulders, I pick my way up niche by niche. Somewhere behind, a spinifex pigeon creaks away, startled. A stone clanks against a hard surface and I hang there, unsure whether I've kicked it loose or flushed something big from a hiding place. I see nothing, hear only wind. Finally I clamber onto a broad ledge beneath a sandstone overhang.

The cave is the size of a child's bedroom. Its rear wall is tawny where the ceaseless southerly has reamed it. When I see the roos folded down on their joints in the chalky dirt I give out a little squawk of surprise. But they do not stir. They lie curved against one another, pooled head to haunch in a rest that seems regal, even holy. I pause a few moments, taking it in. Then I step up and squat before them, peering closely. They really do look as if they're sleeping. But their hides are almost translucent, like the vellum of medieval manuscripts. Tan and grey, shapely even in death, their bodies have been mummified by the high desert air. There's a musky smell but it's not the scent of death, for all about them, like signs of tribute, are the scuffs and scat of the living. Clearly others visit regularly, hunker in the shade beside them and doze through the hottest hours with the breeze rifling through the scalloped chamber. The sun tracks across the cave walls where wasps have daubed candle niches and gargoyles but the mummies seem to lie in perpetual shade here on their soft bed of talc.

I can't help but think of these grand creatures, emblems of our strange island, hauling themselves up here to die, sensing it in their bellies like the shapeless ache of hunger, coming as they've always come to rest in their eyrie above reef and plain. Here they are, still themselves, still beautiful, the wind in their faces, higher than the raptors, above the snakes of the spinifex and the turtles in their rookeries on the beaches far below, like an ancient, priestly caste keeping vigil even in death.

Land of flowers

Since European settlement many parts of this continent have been routinely dismissed as wasteland. Up until twenty years ago Cape Range was one of them. So was my home turf, the triangular swathe of country between Geraldton and Esperance. Even now I hear it called 'rubbish country' because it's so infertile and resistant to Eurocentric notions of beauty. At the friable, windblown western edge, the contours are modest, beaten down, scoured by gales. The climate is Mediterranean but the rainfall is increasingly unreliable. From the limestone reefs and white beaches to the grey and yellow sands of the coastal plain, it's usually dry and gritty. If anything, the country beyond that is harsher still. Visitors like the coast well enough, but they find the interior unappealing. For half the year I live in the margin, between sea and interior, in a district of tawny cap-rock, sandy tracks and grasstrees.

The low grey scrubby heath that people often turn their noses up at is called kwongan – it's akin to Californian chaparral or the fynbos of South Africa. At its coolest coastal periphery, this country is fragrant with olearia and it bristles with hairy spinifex whose tumbleweeds snag in sedges and the flowering scaevola downwind. In the lee of the dunes mats of succulent pigface and Rottnest daisies thrive, but only a few hundred metres inland conditions are harder and hotter and the vegetation is rough and spiny. Bereft of the cooling sea breeze, the valleys are stifling but they grow thick with zamias and spear-headed grasstrees that predate the rise of mammals.

It's tough country to move through. The plants are

armoured and tick-infested. Clenching sprawls of banksia repel walkers with sandpaper bark and breadknife leaves. But there's plenty to see, if you're game. Big western grey kangaroos lounge together in the precious shade of *Callitris* and thickets of gnarly moort. Like scorched shrubs afoot, scruffy emus traverse the ridges in single file. The wattlebirds are brash jokers murdering spiders and moths with casual glee. Goannas appear metallic, galvanized by sun; inert as bush junk, they stir when you encroach, holding their ground, flashing their gums like drunks eager to brawl. At rare, hidden soaks, sheltered by stockades of dirty-shanked paperbarks, tiger snakes laze between feasts of bush mice. Overhead honeyeaters lace the air in pursuit of insects and new blossoms.

Apart from the lurid blue of the sky, the dominant summer colours seem relentlessly austere: khaki on grey over charcoal. But as the autumn arrives you begin to see the arcane spectrum of greens within the foliage. In winter there's white-green, grey-green, orange-green, turmeric-green. Out in the farthest distance, as if suspended in an ether of melaleuca breath, an intense blue-green haze softens the demarcation between land and sky, and at times this looks overworked, a bit artificial, as if added with a spray gun by some addled stoner who couldn't resist a final flourish. In spring the wattles hum yellow. Pigface beds are studded with gaudy pink blossoms. And later, as summer arrives again, the heavy finger-flowers of *Nuytsia floribunda* transform the frumpiest tree on the plain into golden glory. All year the white noise of cicadas is matched by the working drone of bees in a trillion tree blossoms and wildflowers.

No, you wouldn't call it picturesque. At first glance the old home range looks parched, monochrome, monotonous, and upon returning from a holiday somewhere lush, some locals feel downhearted looking out at it. It's always been hard to approach and difficult to understand. Even Charles Darwin struggled to come to terms with it.

In colonial days, explorers climbed points of elevation to 'see what lay before them'. They captured it with their maps. By simply being there, by the act and acquisitive intention of their looking, they claimed it for empire, and in the two centuries since settlement this deep-rooted colonizing instinct endures among those who regard landscape as property, territory, tenement. Otherwise it's open space, a species of vacancy, another form of untapped potential awaiting discovery and exploitation. The implication of such a mindset is that there is no intrinsic value to the earth beneath our feet. Any status must be conferred by an enterprising human and the only standard he or she will recognize is market price, which, despite sounding rational and authoritative, is based on ephemeral and arbitrary perceptions and therefore subject to fluctuation, or what the market touchingly calls 'wildness'.

Often, it's the market value assigned to land that most devalues it. A classic example of this applies here in the south-west corner of Western Australia. This area, the size of England, was once an uninterrupted combination of kwongan heathland and native woodlands unlike any other in the world. But the soils of this great triangle of country are remarkably infertile and were considered useless. That is, of course, until the arrival of superphosphate. Once the magic dust turned up, government agencies and farmers waged what long-serving Director of Agriculture for the state, George Sutton, proudly declared 'a war on the wilderness'. He admitted that 'in common with other wars, there have been some casualties which are greatly regretted. But it has been an achievement in statesmanship, in courage and energy comparable with anything of a like nature in history.'[11] Sutton is remembered for producing a new standard for wheat. Before this, 'Fair Average Quality' was the best the nation could aspire to. But thanks to western vim and a bit of innovation, the market could look to the purity and superiority of 'WA White'. A more emblematic name could scarcely be imagined.

Agricultural warriors and generals like Sutton oversaw the transformation of enormous swathes of land. Once it was cleared this 'waste country' became the mighty West Australian Wheatbelt, as famous a grain-growing hub as Ukraine, a national asset and a source of pride. Over the decades, agriculturalists pressed further into the semi-arid transitional country beyond, and its value too rose from 'rubbish' to 'arable'. But then the soils were beset by salination, a direct effect of all that land-clearing, and rainfall began the steady downward trend it's been in ever since. Broadscale wheatlands lost value and whole tranches have proven themselves toxic investments, to be shed as quickly and quietly as possible. The communities that sprang up mid-century are shrinking steadily. Broadacre farming is now so heavily mechanized it's a neglible source of employment. Western Australia is still a major grain producer but its dependence upon chemical inputs only increases and its exposure to drought remains acute. Along the eastern fringe few operations are profitable and throughout the whole Wheatbelt, in a farming cohort that is aging and sometimes bewildered, rates of suicide are infamous.

Without underlying intrinsic value, the preciousness of land is momentary and destructive. A brief flurry of interest transforms negative space into prime country and then leaves it positively worthless. Consider the city-sized pits, the slagheaps and arsenic ponds of all the played-out mines on this continent. There are no wastelands in our landscape quite like those we've created ourselves.

Of course great slabs of Australia have been dismissed as badlands without any help from the market or human endeavour. It's not uncommon, even in the twenty-first century, to hear the continent's interior referred to as its 'dead heart'. It seems that despite what we have learnt about the ecology of arid ecosystems, this cultural trope never fades. Closer to the coast, not far from our cities, some of them toiling on gamely with the life support that desal plants afford, the Eurocentric view of earlier times still deems immensely rich and unique ecosystems to be 'rubbish country'.

Happily, though, the kwongan heath region of the southwest is being rescued from ignominy by botanists and ecologists who've taken the trouble to look more closely, more carefully and more openly at what is present in here. The most prominent of these reformers and rescuers is Professor Stephen Hopper. Former curator of Kew Gardens and the Millennium Seed Bank in London, Hopper is an Australian botanist who specializes in conservation biology. In the 1980s, having grown up with the assumption that the region was sparse and insufferably dull, he and his collaborators began to see this vast tract for what it is – a veritable subcontinent of rare and precious vegetation. What locals had largely looked upon as marginal country turned out to be an island of flowers. This ecoregion is so species-rich it's completely redrawn the botanical status of the area. In subsequent decades, Hopper and many other scientists have come to find that over seven thousand species of higher plants exist here. Half of them are endemic. There are more plant species present per square kilometre than can be found in many rainforests. And every year new species are discovered. The Southwest Australian Floristic Region is now considered one of the world's biodiversity hotspots.[12] This gives it equivalent standing to Brazil's Atlantic Forest and Madagascar's dry deciduous forests. Not only is it home to a singular suite of plants, it is vital habitat for creatures like Carnaby's black cockatoo, Gilbert's potoroo, the woylie, and my old boyhood totem, the western swamp turtle.

On the basis of this, scientists in 2015 began the push to have the ecoregion put forward for World Heritage listing. But even as that happens plans are afoot to clear another two hundred thousand hectares north of Esperance to make way for more agriculture. After the Wilderness Society gained access to documents under Freedom of Information, Steve Hopper expressed his alarm at the development, saying it posed 'a very high risk' to the integrity of this ecosystem. 'We're still finding new species,' he said. 'It just reflects how much more is out there that we don't know about.'[13]

Of the 18.3 million hectares cleared in Western Australia last century, most were here in this refuge between desert and sea. That the region still has 6 million remnant hectares intact in a single continuous swathe is something to be grateful for. And clearly it's something precious that deserves protection from the momentary enthusiasms of the market. Until recently we literally did not know what we had underfoot and all about us. Ignorance and incuriosity made us strangers in our own country. The steady, painstaking work of botanists, ecologists, painters of natural history and photographers has worn a breach in this ignorance. This research isn't only a scientific advance, it's a mental step forward, an emotional deepening.

It takes humility and patience to see what truly lies before us. A different kind of seeing comes, Hopper says, to those who 'stay longer and look with open hearts and minds'. We need not search merely in order to capture. Our fresh gaze yearns to understand, to bring knowledge inward – not just to catalogue it, but to celebrate what we encounter, to nurture and protect it.

Georgiana Molloy (1805–43) is perhaps the classic West Australian example of a newcomer who learnt to see this place with an open heart and mind. A settler in the raw southern outpost of Augusta nearly two centuries ago, she came to this strange country with the tastes and sensibilities of a Georgian lady, an officer's wife. And like other colonists, she found much of what she saw bewildering, even repulsive. She and her neighbours regarded the country as a monotonous wasteland to be dominated and transformed, and a good deal of her pioneering experience was mean drudgery and brutal disappointment. For a woman of her era and class, botanizing was a hobby, something with which to pass the time and gain a little respite from her labours. She began gathering seeds and flowers diffidently. In fact she had to be encouraged by Captain James Mangles, an amateur botanist who asked her to send specimens to him upon his return to England. Mrs Molloy turned out to be an excellent and fastidious collector, although she was not exactly seduced by her environment as some others were. Her epiphany seems to have had its roots in tragedy. Deranged by grief over the death of a child, her mind and her heart were rent open.

During her long recovery she returned to botanizing. She grew more confident, more passionate. She saw 'such flowers of the imagination' that she was transformed. When she followed her husband north to the Vasse district she was aided in her collecting by the knowledge, hospitality and curiosity of Noongars, and many of her later encounters with these people seem to have been a source of pleasure as well as enlightenment. Georgiana Molloy's years of botanizing were brief. She died in her thirties, after the birth of her seventh child. Her collections are still at the herbarium at Kew. They're catalogued under a man's name, James Mangles.

My father was raised at Margaret River and as a kid I grew up playing with my cousins at Vasse, and camping at Augusta. Later, as a teenager and adult, I surfed the beaches and coves of the region every chance I got and felt a real kinship with the place. I was familiar with the Molloy name because of Molloy Island, at the junction of the Blackwood and Scott rivers, but I was thirty-four before I learnt, thanks to William Lines's biography, *An All Consuming Passion*, who Georgiana Molloy was and what she'd done. Hers is not the conventional pioneering story of endurance and triumph. Her legacy is scientific, of course, but her most important contribution is a matter of sensibility. She was an outlier, one of the first and perhaps the most unlikely, among those who saw in this strange new place the sorts of riches that grasping, toiling settlers were to overlook for the best part of two centuries. It seems hard to credit that scientists like Steve Hopper are still finding these treasures and redeeming country from ignorance, contempt and misuse. The gap between what we see and what we know may not be as wide as it once was, but the temptation to assume we know more than we do remains. To many of us country is no longer just real estate. Now and then, thanks to those prophetic voices, we see the world, in the words of David Mowaljarlai, as 'everything standing up alive'.[14]

X

Dodnun, 2006

Chapman's drunk when we arrive to collect him, and my heart sinks. Outside his house in the back streets of Derby his nephews and their mates are reeling. At the kitchen bench, beleaguered but stoical, his wife Dorothy chops meat in a welter of flies while Chapman sits on his bed nearby. He's bare-chested and wizened and it's been many days since he last shaved. He greets us warmly but he looks dazed and a little disoriented. He only dimly remembers our arrangement and seems to have been caught out by our sudden arrival, but Dorothy is unfazed – in fact she's excited in her gravely shy way. They don't have a car and they haven't been back on country for a long while. After a few minutes of oblique and disjointed conversation, Chapman stirs himself, finds a shirt and comes out to the vehicle. If we're truly going, he says, as if he hasn't let himself believe it until now, he'll need to bring his grandson. And so we go searching through the town for the boy, but every house, lane and creekbed we try is a dead end. Chapman is hapless and befuddled, but slowly, over the course of the day, he sobers up, and though he's tired and disheartened some of his characteristic dignity returns. He's keen to find the lad and get on the road, and now he's thinking more clearly our hunt gains a sharper focus, but the day is getting away from us. Eventually, a jaunty urchin with scabies and a paperclip for a toothpick tells us Isaac is at Mowanjum. Given the lateness of the hour we all agree to go out and get him tomorrow. Then we'll head north.

Next morning when we return with an extra Land Cruiser, Chapman's up and ready. The only thing he's carrying for the week away is his tobacco tin. He still looks ragged, but he's clear-headed and full of purpose. Despite her best efforts, Dorothy cannot suppress her delight at the prospect of being homeward bound. She's brought her granddaughter, a pretty, sheepish girl of fourteen. We drive out to Mowanjum, just beyond the outskirts of Derby, where the magnificent boab trees give way once more to acacias and snappy gums. An indigenous community of about three hundred people, it was established after the demise of the Kunmunya Mission in 1956 when the closely allied Ngarinyin, Worora and Wunambal peoples were separated from their ancestral lands in the north Kimberley. Mowanjum is not the traditional home country of these peoples, but after many years of forced removals it has become at least, as the name suggests, 'settled ground'. Just outside the gate, near the highway, the buffel grass glitters with aluminium cans, and a Woolworths bag flaps like a crippled cockatoo at the base of a eucalypt. Halfway down the drive the flash new arts building is almost finished. A five-million-dollar project, it's a source of pride and promise, though for the moment it looks incongruous with the streets and houses that lie trash-strewn and becalmed beyond.

Negotiating car wrecks and twitching dogs, we pay our respects to frail elders and milky-eyed lawmen and as we wend our way from house to house we run into many familiar faces. There are hugs and tears and plenty of gossip. Eventually we locate young Isaac who climbs into the back of the troopy without hesitation. But when we ask if he's had breakfast he just shrugs. Chapman sends him to the canteen and a few minutes later he returns with a pie and a Coke and finally we turn for the highway. Somehow, without conferring on the matter, we've arranged ourselves according to gender – males in one vehicle, females in the other – and as I brake at the turn-off the high, raucous laughter of girls and old ladies carries on the hot wind.

Chapman's first name is Paul, but he usually goes by Chapman or Jadman. He's a short, wiry fellow with an impish sense of humour and he wears his authority lightly. In towns and roadhouses, where whitefellas run everything, he's just an inconsequential little old man with enigmatic English, but among the Ngarinyin he's a heavy lawman. He's responsible for certain male initiation rites, but that sort of business isn't up for discussion today. We stick to fishing and hunting and football, which of course in our part of the country can only mean Australian Rules. I'm a Dockers man. Chapman follows the Eagles. For a few kilometres we sledge each other's teams, teasing and laughing good-naturedly, though we agree there are players whose skills surpass any sort of team loyalty, and for nearly an hour we list them off and count their many virtues. The fact that every one of them is a blackfella goes unremarked.

As a younger man Chapman worked as a stockman at Mount Elizabeth station, between the Barnett and Hann rivers. Dorothy was there, too. She was a cook and a domestic at the homestead and there's a lovely photo of her in a ghostwritten memoir of those 'pioneering' days that captures her in all her fresh-faced beauty. Few workers would have been closer to the boss and his family than her. For her many years of service she is memorialized as 'an Aboriginal woman', a caption that speaks eloquently of the feudal mindset and the status of indigenous workers when adult men were known as 'boys'. Under the old paternalism Chapman and Dorothy worked for little more than tucker and tobacco, and yet they were still close to country with its precious sustaining power, and like many indigenous veterans of that era in the Kimberley, they're wistful about it. Those days began to come to an end in the late 1960s. When pastoralists were finally forced to pay their labourers a decent wage, Aborigines and their families were no longer welcome. That was when Rolf Harris's 1957 song

'Tie Me Kangaroo Down Sport' had a weird and shameful currency, for right across the country, station owners were setting their 'abos' loose now that they were no longer of use.

Paternalism notwithstanding, Chapman loved that old life – the trucks and the mustering, the tucker and the hunting. He misses the horses the most, and although he doesn't come right out and say so plainly, it seems that for all the grotesque inequalities, he also misses the relative certainty and purpose of that time.

Chapman is a countryman of the late David Mowaljarlai. He's not as well educated in whitefella ways as that legendary statesman was, and his English is sketchy by comparison, but he's deeply literate in his own tradition, a vital carrier of culture. This isn't always fully appreciated by the younger generation of his clan, many of whom, he says, are 'cheeky and wild'. They're caught between worlds, and town life isn't helping. At Mowanjum the youth suicide rate is unimaginable. Mowaljarlai's vision was for the young to flourish in both traditions and this is what Chapman hopes for, but his own experience of two-way living has been a struggle. His culture is ancient and strong and it hangs on despite all odds, but the old people are few and feeble now, and he's tired in himself these days. He'd like to get away from the disorder of Derby and the hectic life at Mowanjum and spend his last years back on country, at the outstation at Dodnun, an excision of Mount Elizabeth. But he's not in the best of health and the nursing post up there has been shut down. The most he can look forward to is a visit now and then to charge up his spirit. He'll be glad to see his home country and some old faces. Scotty and Jordpa will be there. We'll collect Pansy and Morton and Dollund at Mount Barnett, he says, and be at Dodnun by dark. There'll be a big fuss when we roll in. Some youngsters will get a fire going and we'll make plans for a fishing trip down along the Hann River. He says it all timorously, in his husky murmur, as we ride up the blacktop. Slim Dusty comes over the radio and he sings along, all his shyness gone for a moment. He has a fine voice. When you hear him keening plaintively in his own language on Scotty Martin's *Jadmi Junba* you feel the power and certainty of a voice unbowed by time and untouched by modernity.[5]

And then, quite suddenly, the old fellow's spurt of energy wanes. He tucks a wad of tobacco under his lip and lapses into silence. Soon enough he's asleep. Curled against the door he looks as serene as a child.

We jolt down off the sealed highway and hit the rugged

surface of the old Gibb River Road, which is little more than a rocky track riven with potholes, gutters and jaw-rattling corrugations, and in an instant the vehicle behind us is lost in the plume of beige dust we kick up as we pound and wallow along. The troopy shudders and lurches and the coins in the ashtray begin to jingle and leap. But Chapman sleeps on, undisturbed. Across the plain, burnt acacias and spear grass tilt away as if from the force of our approach.

After an hour or so Chapman wakes. And for many kilo-metres he's silent. He doesn't sing along to the radio, not to Slim nor anyone else. He seems subdued, perhaps even a little agitated.

But at the first glimpse of the King Leopold Ranges, as gold as roo fat in the afternoon light, he jerks upright and slaps his thigh like a man who's just won a chook raffle. The boy behind us lets out a little groan of appreciation. We're hours away yet, but these hills mark the beginning of home and now Chapman's laughing, telling jokes I can't quite follow. Minute by minute he grows more animated, until he's transformed. The beaten old wreck I collected in town is a sprightly, bright-eyed man. For him the trip is no sentimental return, it's life support.

As we make the turn for Mount Elizabeth and Dodnun

and ford the first creek, Chapman lashes the side of the Toyota as if to spur us on, and we bound up the farther bank roaring like raiders.

Only five years later, he's gone. When I hear the news I go to the music shelf in sorrow and dig out Scotty's CD and slip it into the machine. And as I listen to Chapman sing, high and strong with his countrymen, I remember him asleep in the soft sand of a creekbed, shaved and handsome in the dappled shade, a man restored. 'When I'm on a high mountain looking out over country,' Mowaljarlai used to say, 'my Unggurr [life-force] flows out from inside my body and I fall open with happiness.'[16]

Paying respect

As a kid from a devout religious family I was always acutely aware of how skittish people could be about anything to do with the sacred. My neighbours and schoolmates did not exactly welcome expressions of spiritual devotion – that sort of thing made them very uncomfortable, even angry – and in this regard, despite two generations of multiculturalism, Australians haven't changed much. We're pretty good at maintaining a secular public space, and that's worth celebrating, but we're a bit tin-eared about matters of religion and anxious about using terms like 'sacred'. This strikes me as a bit ironic, for we live on the most spiritually potent continent imaginable. But apart from family, the only thing sacred to most of us is our much-vaunted 'way of life'. And what is that but an unspecified mixture of political, financial and spatial liberties enjoyed in sunshine at the island's margins? Not even the confected sanctification of Anzac Day can rival it. But the recent recommissioning and deliberate sacralization of the Gallipoli myth is telling, because it suggests a spiritual vacuum, a palpable absence at our core, as if deep down, ordinary folks want to submit to something grand and sublime. But Anzac has been coarsened by the politics of nostalgic regression. It's close to becoming the sort of nationalist death cult we revile when it appears in other places or under a different flag, and I fail to see how such a false sense of the sacred nourishes the individual or the community, because the only thing it sustains is the security of those who send our young men and women to new wars, some of which have proven every bit as pointless and wasteful as the bungled adventure in the Dardanelles in 1915.

These are not easy things to say. Several members of my family were in the 1st AIF. My grandmother's brother died like a good Lighthorseman, watering the nags, shot dead by a Turkish airman. But I don't feel enlarged or enlightened by his death. When I hold his bloodstained wallet with respect and awe I don't get a sacramental, nationalistic charge – all I feel is tragedy and blind waste. I think of a boy's life squandered for jingoistic nonsense. I think of his sister who mourned him for more than seventy years.

While it's true that anything we really value will exact a price, that price has to be worth paying. And what's so precious I'd lay down my life for it? Not the Crown or the state, that's for sure. The first thing I think of as sacred is the bond between parent and child – then spouses and lovers, of course, friends and countrymen, for these are kinships that strengthen our connection to one another and enlarge our lives. To enter wholeheartedly into a relationship is to leave oneself open to being claimed, and held so in perpetuity. That's the power of love. And also its price. No wonder people are sometimes loath to commit. Most of us are better at claiming than being claimed, and when it comes to thinking about land and home this is a hard lesson Australians have been learning since settlement. But after two centuries of demanding and seizing, many non-indigenous Australians have finally begun to commit. Out of reverence, from love, in a spirit of kinship to the place itself. This amounts to a recognition of our settler past and a moving on from what has been an abusive, one-sided relationship in which the island continent gave and we just took. It's a rejection of the retrospective tendency of invaders to mythologize their origins and minimize their outrages. For invasions are what they are and their consequences endure.

Whether our European forebears came in chains or in hope of a new life and fresh opportunities, their arrival was a catastrophe for Aboriginal peoples and for the land itself. Much of this damage will never be undone. Like alien cells entering an organism, newcomers have changed it forever, and we continue to affect it and are in some senses helpless to do otherwise. We are, each of us, at the mercy of what others did before we arrived. An Iraqi immigrant who settles in Australia is no more responsible for the conditions that greet her than her Aboriginal neighbours are for the chaos that caused her to flee her homeland. I feel ancestral shame for the dispossession of this country's first peoples, shame for the despoliation of their lands and a kind of national shame, too, for the mess my nation helped create in Mesopotamia in recent years, but in none of these instances do I feel guilt. None of us is responsible for the culture and social conditions we're born into. But that doesn't mean we're absolved from reflecting upon our inheritance. Neither does our good fortune give licence to mindlessly replicate the settler ethic of two centuries ago.

In so many respects – matters of religion, politics, gender, education – the attitudes of my nineteenth-century forebears are archaic and alien. So much so that I struggle sometimes to feel related – if it were possible for us to meet we'd be utter strangers, mutually incomprehensible – yet by genes, history and collective memory we *are* related and I feel compelled to honour this. Past or present, family will continue to make claims upon me. What should have no claim upon me is the colonial mindset bent toward annexation, enclosure, consolidation and jealous surveillance in defence of territorial gains. It breaks people and ruins places and it shackles the lives and imaginations of those who profit by it. For too long it has retarded Australians' social and spiritual progress; to this day many influential people in business and politics are firmly in its thrall. They dissociate our enviable life of casual prosperity from the natural world that sustains it. Despite what half a century of science has taught us, regardless of the kindred reciprocity many Australians now feel with the land of their birth, these decision-makers are insufficiently mindful of the organic costs of how we live. And this is no longer a question of ignorance – they know full well what the situation is. Their refusal to change is an ideological aversion. No matter how pragmatic they sound, in their dogged attachment to a spurious economy where endless growth and consumption have no real consequences, they display a devotion to magical thinking they seem to find contemptible in others. Theirs is a cult that does not encourage reflection, a faith built on looking forward at all times, a belief system unsettled by the backward glance, because to look back is to acknowledge a trail of destruction – to ecosystems, languages, cultures, entire peoples. Moreover a citizen prospering in the present may discover that most of the sacrifices that paid for this prosperity were made by countrymen and women who were never likely to share in the spoils. Looking inward is even more troubling, because lying in wait for the captain of industry and the political insider is the anxious prospect that he, too, might eventually be required to give something up.

In the centuries since Galileo's explosive new understanding of the cosmos first rattled our cage, humans have never quite managed to give up the idea that we are at the centre of the universe and masters of all we survey. We're used to seeing ourselves as the pinnacle of reality. But travelling deep into landscape, paying attention to the natural world, we're reminded of our true position in the scheme of things. Yes, we are evolutionary inheritors of immense creativity and power, a fundamental terrestrial phenomenon – perhaps, in the words of palaeontologist Pierre Teilhard de Chardin, '*the* fundamental phenomenon of nature' – yet we are, in the end, tiny. Not only in the context of the cosmos, where we hardly have the status of spores, but as dwellers on an island continent like Australia where we are, whether we acknowledge it or not, mere creatures of the earth, vulnerable and dependent.

In an uncompromising landscape like ours, a person suddenly confronted with their essential smallness will often panic, become angry, disoriented, afraid. Out of reflex they'll scramble back into the armoured shell of their pre-eminence: the airconditioned car, the helicopter, the skyscraper, the shopping mall. The quest for an open-minded engagement with nature is as challenging and uncertain for individuals as it is for corporations and communities. Ingrained habits of mind are tenacious and nature is elusive, enigmatic, at times resistant. It's possible some of us will never feel truly at home in Australian land-scapes. There are newcomers arriving every day and sadly many of them will only ever know urban Australia, with its undistinguished architecture and its monotonous replica-tion of the same commercial franchises – the Subways and 7-Elevens and H&R Blocks – that render so many cities of the world largely interchangeable, if not entirely placeless. Whether they're migrants or native-born, some Australians will always invest their affections in the state – Australia the Idea – for so much of contemporary life floats on abstrac-tions and virtualities. But I meet young people all over Australia – from Timber Creek in the Northern Territory to Airlie Beach in the Whitsundays, from the Abrolhos Islands to the Great Ocean Road – who are passionate and curious about this country and who do not hesitate to have it make claims upon them. They're enchanted by the place but they readily concede how often it puzzles them. They're sheepish about how little they know, but then a continent like this is too big and rich and complex to be truly understood. No matter who you are it will always slip through your fingers to some extent. Sometimes I think it's sufficient to admit you're mystified, not just because it's an honest response, but because it's a suitably humble one. For all the empirical knowledge we've garnered, and the many generations of lived experience that resonate in our collective memory, this continent remains an enigma. It's been a haven for humans for millennia and yet it is not humanized as other continents are. Submitting to its scale, acknowledging its irrepressible particularities, listening for its cryptic music and seeking to learn its ways enriches us. We are in a relationship with the land and the conditions of any other relationship apply. My settler ancestors who fenced and farmed what appeared to be wilderness would probably have seen themselves as proprietors and guardians of places. Their relationship to the land was sternly parental. Australians of my generation, and those younger than me, might be more likely to consider themselves children of the island and this distinction is significant. If we've learnt anything about living in this country it's that we depend upon its health for our sustenance. But the land, like any parent, is large and strange and hard to read. And as the songman Neil Murray reminds us, it will always be there, awaiting our return.

Still, Australia is not completely enshrouded in obscurity. Some of those who know it best are anxious to nurture the rest of us, the new majority, through our long, tottering infancy into a state of informed responsibility. They are the bearers of a vast but now rapidly diminishing reservoir of lore, parts of which they've been waiting to share for many decades. These are citizens who could hardly be blamed for inhabiting and projecting only furious victimhood. Indigenous health statistics and rates of incarceration alone would justify any amount of rage. And yet many Aboriginal Australians are disarmingly stoical. Few seem to envy the lives of their non-indigenous countrymen. In fact there are some notable elders who openly pity any citizen who lacks the richness of traditional culture. They don't see themselves as victims but as carriers of ancient and hardwon knowledge at once philosophically sophisticated and practical. Largely spurned by settlers, ignored by consolidating colonial successors, and either patronized, romanticized or politicized by every generation thereafter, Aboriginal wisdom is the most under-utilized intellectual and emotional resource this country has.

A good deal of Aboriginal culture is arcane and dizzyingly complex to the outsider – many things are secret-sacred and will remain so – and yet the passage of the Native Title Act of 1993 depended upon this kind of knowledge being taken seriously by the highest courts of the land. Never before had non-Aboriginal Australia granted traditional culture such intellectual weight. This shift did not come easily. Not all the outcomes have been fair, or comprehensible to those without advanced law degrees, and many first peoples had their native title recognized only in order to have it traduced, but the fact remains that ancient tradition has begun to exert a material influence on our laws, and it has altered our broader national narrative for all time. That's no small thing. But it strikes me as tragic that this knowledge and its transformative outlook have not yet found their way more deeply into the popular mind. I'm not sure this can be explained away as the result of racism alone. To me it also smacks of the defensive, self-hating contempt some Australians still nurse for the local product. The philosophies, medicine and spritual practices of exotic cultures have been quick to gain status in recent decades. They aren't just respectable – they're bankable. Some of that may be because they're sound and fruitful outlooks. Some of it is simply the glamour and allure of exotica. Perhaps the simplest and most profound lesson to be learnt from Aboriginal lawmen and women is that the relationship to country is corporeal and familial. We need a more intimate acquaintance with the facts. We need to feel them in our bodies and claim them and belong to them as if they were kin. This has political implications, of course, but it also offers an ethical and emotional deepening that may enrich the lives of millions. That was the view of the visionary Ngarinyin lawman David Banggal Mowaljarlai.

Born in 1925 on the Kimberley coast, Mowaljarlai lived a traditional life but he also had a mission education at Kunmunya and he became an adept in both cultures. Photographed as a small bright-eyed boy by the first European anthropologists to visit the far north-west in the 1930s, he went on to distinguish himself as a young man of extraordinary intelligence. He trained as a Presbyterian lay minister and was later an ambulance driver, a lugger engineer, a painter, a social justice advocate and a land-rights activist. A handsome man and a charismatic speaker of great eloquence, he travelled all over the world in his subsequent role as storyteller, thinker and educator. He established himself as one of the greatest unsalaried ambas-sadors Australia ever produced. His fervent desire was to have Aboriginal children equipped to prosper in the irrevo-cably altered conditions of post-invasion Australia and he did whatever he could to present the ancient wisdom of his own tradition to whitefellas, who didn't have a clue what they were missing. 'We are really sorry for you people,' he said in one of his many broadcasts. 'We cry for you because you haven't got meaning of culture in this country. We have a gift we want to give you. We keep getting blocked from giving you that gift. We get blocked by politics and politicians. We get blocked by media, by process of law. All we want to do is come out from under all this and give you this gift. And it's the gift of pattern thinking. It's the culture which is the blood of this country, of Aboriginal groups, of the ecology, of the land itself.'[17]

Mowaljarlai's lasting influence on scientists, artists, theologians, literary scholars, anthropologists and jurists is not as well known as it should be. In his final years he threw all his energies into the project of Two-Way Thinking, a philosophy of mutual respect, mutual curiosity and cultural reciprocity. He was the inspiration behind the Bush University initiative that took many non-Aboriginal leaders and lawmakers onto Ngarinyin country in order to expose them to traditional folkways, something which has continued since his death in 1997. Having grown up in a culture still intact and vibrant he saw his clan dispossessed and then shunted from one settlement to another, and in later years his immediate family was beset by despair, alienation and addiction. Even in the midst of two decades of political and legal struggle for the restoration of lands to his countrymen, he made time to offer his knowledge to anyone who'd listen respectfully and plenty who didn't, and he did much of this in his old age. Only since his death has it become clear what he has given to this country, and what he might have achieved had the blockages he despaired of not been so stubborn. He was an immensely talented man who could have prospered had he not taken up the burden of being a conduit between cultures. Those closest to him believe he wore himself out. There are others like him still battling to make themselves heard, though few with his imagination and authority.

Decades before 'mutual obligation' became a catch-phrase beloved of politicians, Mowaljarlai was advancing it as a uniting principle that applied to much more than the benighted recipients of welfare. Two-way living is founda-tional, it springs from the earth itself. It should apply in the boardrooms of telcos and miners and bankers, be embod-ied in our personal and collective decision-making, for the ethic acknowledges the organic facts of life that underwrite all human endeavours.

I'm not an optimist by nature but I'm heartened by the attitudes of many young Australians I meet on forest tracks, beaches or in activist meetings. Their thinking about the natural world and the fragility of life is far more advanced than most of the politicians who represent them in par-liament. They're more widely travelled than their parents. Having backpacked through the US and Europe and Asia, they've been to the future and they don't like what they see. If they're passionate about the natural world it's because they understand they live in a country where there are still things to be saved and treasured. They're proud of that, they take it seriously. If they're impatient about government inaction over climate change, for instance, it's because they know they'll inherit its most bitter fruits.

I think people everywhere yearn for connection, to be overwhelmed by beauty. Maybe, deep down, people need to feel proper scale. Perhaps in the face of grandeur we silently acknowledge our smallness, our bit-part in majesty. Teilhard de Chardin, a Jesuit of heretical optimism, declared that 'terrestrial thought is becoming conscious that it constitutes an organic whole, endowed with the power of growth, and both capable of and responsible for some future'.[18]

Our future *is* organic and material. This earth is our home, our only home. And if home and family aren't sacred, what else can be? The dirt beneath our feet is sacred. Every other consideration springs from this and you don't need to be an archaeologist, a botanist or geologist to know it. Kakadu elder Big Bill Neidjie was none of these. He'd been a buffalo hunter, luggerman and mill worker in his younger days. He was the last surviving speaker of the

Gaagudju language and in his later life he was an inspirational leader, a transitional figure like Mowaljarlai. He wasn't just the father of Kakadu National Park; to my mind he was a mystic. Here, surely, is a voice we should attend to.

> *I love it tree because e love me too.*
> *E watching me same as you*
> *tree e working with your body, my body,*
> *e working with us.*
> *While you sleep e working.*
> *Daylight, when you walking around, e work too.*
>
> *That tree, grass . . . that all like our father.*
> *Dirt, earth, I sleep with this earth.*
> *Grass . . . just like your brother.*
> *In my blood in my arm this grass.*
> *This dirt for us because we'll be dead,*
> *we'll be going this earth.*
> *This the story now.*[19]

Our story is written in the longing of a boy seeing his homeland from exile, in the slow awakening of a grieving woman consoled and stirred by strange flowers, in the dogged curiosity of a botanist returning to a scorned place to find it wasn't what he thought it was. And it's there in the rebellious spirit of no-hopers and heretics standing in front of bulldozers, and in the shining face of an old man looking out upon the ranges of his ancestral country with a heart full to bursting.

Notes

1. William J. Lines, *False Economy*, Fremantle Arts Centre Press, Fremantle, 1998, p 280.

2. Ibid., p 282.

3. Georgiana Molloy, quoted in William J. Lines, *An All Consuming Passion*, Allen & Unwin, Sydney, 1994, p 137.

4. D.H. Lawrence, *Kangaroo*, Penguin Books, Melbourne, 1982, p 87.

5. Peter Ferguson, 'Anti-environmentalism and the Australian culture war', *Journal of Australian Studies*, 33: 289–304. DOI: 10.1080/14443050903079680.

6. Anthony Trollope, quoted in Suzanne Falkiner, *Wilderness*, Simon & Schuster, Sydney, 1992.

7. Tom Griffiths, *Hunters and Collectors*, Cambridge University Press, Cambridge, 1996, p 104.

8. Hannah Rachel Bell, 'All is not as it seems', paper presented at 'Gwion Gwion Rock-art of the Kimberley: Past, Present and Future', University of Western Australia, 14–15 October, 2010. Also cited in Martin Porr and Hannah Rachel Bell, '"Rock-art", "animism" and two-way thinking: towards a complementary epistemology in the understanding of material culture and "rock-art" of hunting and gathering people', *Journal of Archeological Method and Theory*, 19(1): 161-205. DOI: 10.1007/s10816-011-9105-4.

9. Anthony Redmond, 'Some initial effects of pursuing and achieving native title recognition in the northern Kimberley', *The Social Effects*

of Native Title: Recognition, Translation, Coexistence (eds. Benjamin R. Smith and Frances Morphy), Australian National University e-Press, 2007.

10. Lang Hancock, quoted in Michael Coyne and Leigh Edwards, *The Oz Factor: Who's Doing What in Australia*, Dove, East Malvern, 1990, p 68.

11. George Sutton, quoted in William. J. Lines, *Patriots: Defending Australian Natural Heritage*, University of Queensland Press, Brisbane, 2006, p 12.

12. Stephen Hopper and Paul Gioia, 'The Southwest Australian Floristic Region: evolution and conservation of a global hot spot of biodiversity', *Annual Review of Ecology, Evolution and Systematics,* 35: 623–650. DOI: 10.1146/annurev.ecolsys.35.112202.130201.

13. Jake Sturmer, 'Great Western Woodlands: Fears over proposal to release 500,000 hectares of reserve for farming', ABC News, 8 December 2014. At: abc.net.au/news/2014-12-08/fears-over-proposal-to-release-500000-hectares-of-wa-woodland/5950072.

14. David Mowaljarlai and Jutta Malnic, *Yorro Yorro: Aboriginal Creation and the Renewal of Nature,* Inner Traditions, Rochester, Vermont, 1993, p 79.

15. Nyalgodi Scotty Martin, *Jadmi Junba*, Rouseabout Records, 2003.

16. 'Obituary: David Banggal Mowaljarlai', *Journal of Australian Archaeology*, 1997, 45: 58.

17. David Banggal Mowaljarlai, 'An address to the white people of Australia', ABC Radio: *The Law Report*, 1995.

18. Pierre Teilhard de Chardin, *Toward the Future*, Harcourt, Brace Jovanovich, 1975, p 13.

19. Bill Neidjie, *Story About Feeling*, Magabala Books, Broome, 1989, p 4.

Other works referred to

Bell, Hannah Rachel, *Men's Business, Women's Business*, Inner Traditions International, Vermont, 1998.

——*Storymen*, Cambridge University Press, Melbourne, 2009.

Birch, Charles, *On Purpose,* New South Wales University Press, Sydney, 1990.

Cunningham; Irene, *The Land of Flowers: An Australian Environment on the Brink,* Otford Press, 2005.

Flannery, Tim, *The Future Eaters,* Reed Books, Melbourne, 1994.

Grishin, Sasha, *John Wolseley: Land Marks,* Craftsman House, Sydney, 1998.

Lines, William J., *Taming the Great South Land,* Allen & Unwin, Sydney, 1991.

Main, Barbara York, *Between Wodjil and Tor,* Jacaranda Press, Brisbane, and Landfall Press, Perth, 1967.

Nash, Roderick, *Wilderness and the American Mind,* Yale University Press, New Haven, 1973.

Olsen, John, *Drawn from Life,* Duffy & Snellgrove, Sydney, 1997.

Ryan, Simon, *The Cartographic Eye*, Cambridge University Press, Melbourne, 1996.

Serventy, Carol, and Harris, Alwen, *Rolf's Walkabout,* Reed Books, Sydney, 1971.

Serventy, Vincent, *Vincent Serventy: An Australian Life,* Fremantle Arts Centre Press, Fremantle, 1999.

Stockton, Eugene, *The Aboriginal Gift: Spirituality for a Nation,* Millennium Books, Alexandria, New South Wales, 1996.

Wright, Judith, *The Coral Battleground,* Thomas Nelson (Australia) Ltd, Melbourne, 1977.

Acknowledgments

Island Home had its beginnings in a collaboration with the photographer Richard Woldendorp and the essay 'Strange Passion' that accompanied his 1999 book, *Down to Earth*. 'The Island Seen and Felt' was first given as a talk at the Royal Academy, London in 2013 and was published in *Illumination: The Art of Philip Wolfhagen* in 2013. A later version also appeared in *The Australian* in 2014. 'Cape Range, 2009' was published as 'The Cave' in *The Australian Colour Magazine* in 2014.

Grateful acknowledgment is made to the following for permission to quote: Meredith McKinney for Judith Wright's 'The Surfer', *Collected Poems*, HarperCollins; 'My Island Home', words and music by Neil Murray, © Universal Music Publishing Pty Ltd, all rights reserved, international copyright secured, reprinted with permission; the estate of Bill Neidjie for *Story About Feeling*, Magabala Books.

Hank Kordas

The preeminent Australian writer of his generation, Tim Winton is the author of twenty-eight books. His work is translated into twenty-eight languages and has been adapted for stage and screen. He has won the Miles Franklin Award four times (for *Shallows*, *Cloudstreet*, *Dirt Music*, and *Breath*) and has twice been short-listed for the Booker Prize (for *The Riders* and *Dirt Music*). Long active in the environmental movement in Australia, and patron of the Australian Marine Conservation Society, he was listed as a National Living Treasure in 1997. He lives in Western Australia.

milkweed
editions

Founded as a nonprofit organization in 1980, Milkweed Editions
is an independent publisher. Our mission is to identify, nurture
and publish transformative literature, and build
an engaged community around it.

milkweed.org